Year of the Dog
A Poet's Journal

April Bulmer

Copyright © 2021 by April Bulmer

All rights reserved. No part of this work covered by the copyrights hereon may be reproduced or used in any form or by any means – graphic, electronic or mechanical, including photocopying, recording, taping or information storage and retrieval systems – without the prior written permission of the publisher.

Library and Archives Canada Cataloguing in Publication

CIP data on file with the National Library and Archives

ISBN e-book edition 978-1-55483-486-0
ISBN trade paperback edition 978-1-55483-485-3

Acknowledgments

I am grateful to the Ontario Arts Council for their generous funding through their Recommender Grants for Writers program. Special thanks to Black Moss Press, Hamilton Arts & Letters and Insomniac Press who recommended me for these grants.

I would also like to thank the Bernice Adams Bursary committee in Cambridge, Ontario for awarding me funds.

Thank you to members and former members of the Cambridge Writers Collective who read the manuscript and offered thoughtful suggestions.

I also wish to thank friends and family who support me in a variety of ways and editors who have published my work through the years.

"Fish" and "The Colour Purple" appeared in *Synaeresis Issue 5*, "Poppies" on the Cambridge Writers Collective Website, "Native Tongue" in *Prairie Clan*, "O Holy Night" in *The Second Genesis: An Anthology of Contemporary World Poetry*, "Rowell Jackman Hall" in *Devour: Art & Lit Canada Issue 002*, "Full Moon" in *The Magic Happens*, an early version of "Roots" in *Transition*, "Cousin" in *Arc*, "Saints," "Mute" and "Beautiful Tune" in *Dancing on Stones*, "Shang Dynasty" and "Wax and Wane" in *Beneath a Hallowed Moon: A Mystical-Magical Anthology of Verse*, "Song" in *Verse Afire*, "Sack," "Canes," "The Balm," "Golden Rules," and "Predictions" in *Setu May 2019*, "Hospital Policies" in *Open Minds*, "World Poetry Day," "Homily" and "Saints" in *Devour: Art & Lit Canada Issue 008*, "Buffalograss," "Sacraments," and "Scar Tissue" in *Hearthbeat; Poems of Family and Hometown*, "Hindu Temple" in *The Beauty of Being Elsewhere* and "Ocular Eye Clinic," "Breath," "Body of Christ," "Queen of Wands," "Frames" and "The Rock" in *True Identity*.

Year of the Dog: A Poet's Journal was shortlisted for the 2019 International Beverly Prize for Literature. My thanks to the judges and to Eyewear Publishing for their support.

The privilege of a lifetime is being who you are.

Joseph Campbell

Foreword

I am a poet who has written for 40 years in sloppy journals. I attempted tidier, more coherent entries during the Chinese Year of the Dog (February 16, 2018 – February 4, 2019). This was a period that promised opportunities to those of us who set goals, followed our hearts and maintained a positive attitude. Themes unfolded naturally and tended to be spiritual, psychological and romantic, reflecting my past as well as my present.

I was born in Toronto, Canada in 1963 and shortly after moved to the suburb of Mississauga where I remained until I graduated from York University at age 23. I am an only child and was raised in a lovely, wooded neighbourhood called Sherwood Forest.

Thanks to my parents' generosity and support, I eventually obtained Master's degrees in religious studies and theological studies, as well as creative writing. Writing poetry became a passion that brought light to dim days and allowed me to investigate a variety of doctrines and practices. Raised Anglican and having spent a year in Divinity school, I maintain an interest in the Church and its beautiful rituals, but my old soul speaks loudly about exploring other forms of worship and belief. While difficult to defend in an academic setting, this 'syncretic' system offers me a little peace. As a result, I wrote a book (*Creeds and Remedies: The Feminine and Religion in Waterloo Region,* Serengeti Press, 2017) on various religions practiced by women in Waterloo Region, where I have lived for more than 25 years. Feminist principles and new ways for women to express their spiritual instincts also became a recurrent theme in my poetry, and I wrote a book about women worshipping by the Grand River in Cambridge, Ontario. There they expressed their deepest truths in the presence of a High Priestess.

"Imagine the fertile womb, the goddess of river and earth, the moonlight and menses of prayer, the dimming of darkness with light, the flowering of candle in flame, the trimmed wick and the softening wax of its burning, the communion of alluvial soil and bursting seed, the flow of healing waters, the slaking of spiritual thirst, the blooming of life and the crossing of shadows and shades of the grave and you have entered the world of Bulmer's lovely metaphysical poetry where the metaphysics are simplified by the clarity of luminous lines," wrote Poet Laureate John B. Lee in the preface to my *Out of Darkness, Light* (Hidden Brook Press, 2018). About this same book, poet Katherine L. Gordon wrote: "So much of woman, her qualities, desires, special attributes, has been hidden in cultural darkness, long stifled by dogma and prejudice. This light that April Bulmer brings to us from that long tenebrae rises to a sanctified space where the feminine soul can at last inhabit and display."

Year of the Dog: A Poet's Journal, however, does not only embrace my love of spirituality, religion and culture but exposes some of my experiences living in a variety of Canadian cities including Toronto and Montreal, Windsor and Cambridge, Ontario. I hope it speaks to anyone who is interested in some biographical details of a woman who lost her beloved Shih Tzu in the Year of the Dog and who is committed to her craft. Through diary entries, short essays, prose and poems it reflects my eccentric, poetic nature.

February 16, 2018
Cataract

My mother's right eye: a dirty windshield. The nurse offers three white pills. She is Meghan, a pretty redhead. Soon, my mother babbles like a child. She lies down on a stretcher in Bay 19. The iodine drops sting, stain her face and hair.

I sip peppermint tea in the waiting room. Across, a handsome man wears a small gold earring and a wedding band. He avoids my 20/20 stare.

Another nurse escorts my mother into a wheelchair. "Your limousine awaits," he says. She wears a plastic shield on the eye. Her face is pale and fallen.

Tonight, a new moon, a foggy sky.

February 21, 2018
Gynecology

Winter rain. Grand River floods.

Ainslie Automotive. My little blue car: a kind of Pap test.

February 23, 2018
Patron Saint of Travellers

Rain again. Grand River high. CBC Radio in my little blue car: *Canada Live*. I was a Toronto gal. Today I am in Galt, in the south end of Cambridge. I hold a wee medallion of St. Christopher, baby Jesus on his shoulders.

I will travel to you in the night, my spirit and silver cord. Rest with you, C—, then rise in the morn. Stroke your hair with a wide-tooth comb, for you have grown it long; tinted the shade of tea tree. You are young and punk. I am crone. My hair is grey at the temples. I pray you visit *me* in the dim. I am a woman now but often alone.

We might motor together in my car, St. Christopher swinging from the rearview mirror.

February 26, 2018
Snowdrops

Wind yesterday and the moisture is gone.

My dog is sleepy and retires after a short walk.

In the shower, I squeeze my shampoo bottle. It whines. I imagine I bear your child, C—. Perhaps it is manic like your father and mine, or depressed as I was in Windsor, a border town.

Today, I dance — Nia class. I open like a snowdrop in weak winter light. I might offer myself to you: a small flower blooms in hard earth — despite.

February 27, 2018
Chin

My Shih Tzu and I walk the river in the sun.

How tired I am. Rose at 5 a.m. in the dim. Slept poorly. Dreamed of

Chin again. Perhaps I knew him in past lives. He is mostly Chinese, I think, and prone to suicide.

Chin is my shadow. He is small and poorly groomed. A wild tint of red hair, but quiet and still mentally ill.

The wind howls. The dog's fur a cowl. Chin coughs and shivers in the chill.

February 28, 2018
Queen of Wands

I dream of you, J—. You walk with a cane.

On Saturday: a fortune teller again. She will read the tarot, my chart and the lines on my palm: the geography of love and fate.

Remember, we were girls at the Cozy Tea Room on Gerrard? A man behind a velvet drape read my wristwatch, a well-worn ring. Promised a career in TV.

You wrote novels, won awards, married, bore a blonde girl — a photographer who shoots for *Vogue*.

I worked for TVOntario; care for an elderly mom, a sickly dog, my own wounds. Pen little poems about the feminine God and Her battered earth, Her runes. For I am Taurus, Virgo Moon.

March 1, 2018
Subcultures

I open the portal of my mind, and it creaks. A cobweb, its quaint crotchet. How punk you are C— there in the dim light. Your black leather jacket, a hand-painted emblem on the back: Lord of Chaos and a symbol I don't understand.

Your hair is the black of shoeshine, long and gathered at the nape. Your shadow at my door. I fumble with my skirt. It is green. Your dark eyes lower to the place I bleed.

You knock and mumble a greeting and my heart beats. It is a quiet one despite its grief and its murmur. Haunted really like a room with a presence.

You tell me your father is abusive to women. He was the man who kicked me to the curb in Windsor. How I drove nights in my little beige car, an old Spirit. My Yorkshire Terrier, Bear, balanced on a hillock of clothes. He whined a little.

Freighters passed us on the Detroit River bearing their own heavy loads. How the water buoyed their weight.

March 2, 2018
Malware

I wait for my computer, infected and down. I want to message you C— though you never respond, turn your cyber-back to me, your virtual warlock hair.

Jupiter retrograde soon: I wish to trace the emblem on your leather jacket again: "Lord of Chaos" — God or Demon?

March 3, 2018
Circus

A belly dancer. His turban peacock blue. He shakes his big gut. I admire Lucy Hoop who juggles fire, the magician who makes a crystal ball float. The man in Chinese togs who offers me a pull from his deck of cards. Even the yellow python like a great rope. A ringmaster, a contortionist, a ballerina *en pointe*. And me, a plump poet, dressed in black dress and print pashmina, vanishes suddenly inside a shawl of night.

March 4, 2018
Mad Hatter

I wrote this poem for a Mad Hatter party held by the Cambridge Writers Collective. We created poetry or prose based on *Alice Through the Looking-Glass* by Lewis Carroll.

Wax and Wane

I fall through the mother space.
Crawl from her on hands and knees.
I live among the mushrooms now:
their soft, moist pleats.
I take one in my teeth
and my eyes are as big as beetles.
A caterpillar like a drop of rain on a leaf.
A mad man so nervous
his cup of tea trembles.
My heart is a deck of cards.

I play the Queen of Hearts.
Her hair the shade of blood.
At night even the moon dreams
it waxes and wanes.
How it swells and shrinks
on currant cake and drugs.

March 6, 2018
Face

A selfie for my new collection of poetry. I study my face. The chicken-pox scar between my eyes: a divine tattoo. Dark circles like half moons. The round cheeks I inherited from Grandma Rete. The little chin. The big teeth. The curly hair I offer to wind and snow and a straw hat in spring. The shadow of my father as I gained weight. The full lower lip my mother read like a gypsy. "Taurus," she said, "you like to eat."

March 7, 2018
Massage

I imagine the therapist holds my mother's pain, discards it into the spiritual realm. It is a shade of red. Massage, effleurage…The deep touch my father rarely gave. Warm oil, hot stones…

A perfect cobweb hangs from a high light in the waiting room where I sit. I think of Jesus. Outside, a wet snow. Justin Bieber sings "Love Yourself." Later, I rub my toes.

March 8, 2018
Blood Relative

My Shih Tzu is ill, her lymph glands swollen. I pray she lives. Vet orders an expensive test. I am a barren woman. I nurse dog to health again and again.

Her soft face lifts to mine. I stroke her fur as vet ties tourniquet. Draws blood from her little white paw.

We are soulmates: a life in China. My teat: a baby girl.

March 9, 2018
Cambridge Memorial Hospital

The Grand River moves fast today. The banks are swollen and sexy. A nest in the groin of a tree. Inside, I sip peppermint tea at Tim Hortons in the basement. The cup warms my chapped hands.

Later, I gather motion of water, energy of winter robin. Anoint you, sad doctor, from a distance with witchy meds.

March 10, 2018
Shadows

My Jungian analyst, her dream: a vessel of blood. Another, a therapist, her addiction to hot dogs.

My own shadow quivers like the Speed River in March. Mute when Father W— broke the host that was my heart. How he played a little organ music, and I could not sing. Then I met a man who suffered too.

His little sweat at Bubi's Awesome Eats in Windsor: a napkin to his damp brow. How I loved him for a time until my dream: his wife! A French gal who had lost a child.

The ring I found in a pocket of his dark jeans. The alchemy of gold.

March 11, 2018
Altar Guild

It is Sunday. I tidy and clean. Fold soft "blankies" from a heap. Remember Bear, my Yorkie. How I covered him as he lay dying: diabetes and other diseases. Blessed his ashes when he passed. His sack of coats and sweaters. His Libra coin and collar. A bowl of cold water.

March 13, 2018
Theatre Arts

I dream of Laudenbach, high-school theatre-arts teacher. Dream, too, of the Montreal poets I knew. The unconscious speaks in symbols, is concerned with a costume party, a fundraiser for local arts at Hamilton Family Theatre in Galt. A performance of *Hairspray*. I will wear a wig, describe my new book to the audience. I will sport saddle shoes. I have created flyers for *Out of Darkness, Light*, an image of hands bearing Goddess healing energy. Mine will, no doubt, perspire at the mic.

March 18, 2018
Lichee

My Shih Tzu's belly is infected, inflamed. She wears a cone around her neck. I call it her Easter bonnet. I bathe her in oatmeal and aloe, swab her with warm water and a cloth. I anoint her, wrap her in soft fabric, as though dying guardian of Kuan Yin, Goddess of Compassion.

March 19, 2018
Moon Blood

I am interested in the spiritual implications of menstruation.

Women of the Cloth

She here among us.
A river between the thighs
of her women.
She has come
for their burden
of moon blood.

How slow I am.
My belly, its weight.
The rags I turn
in a wash of blue suds.

We touched Christ's garments
but he could not heal
our ache.
We were mules
bearing his love.

She is sister.
We are of her cloth:
stained and rubbed.

March 20, 2018
Dragon City

First day of spring, the geese celebrate. The sun gathers strength, though I am weak.

I eat a great feed of Chinese food: lo mein, fried rice and an egg roll at a strip mall in Galt. I like the Asian guy at the cash, his great black glasses and Canadian speak. I wonder if he would be interested in me. How I would swell on a diet of chicken balls, chow mein, vats of wonton soup. Might turn to Buddha, pray for enlightenment, as he did under the Bodhi Tree. Leave a fortune cookie at his feet.

March 21, 2018
World Poetry Day

The body we rent from God. How we are obliged to care for it, wash with a fragrant bar of soap, shampoo the hair. Exercise the body as though a slim dog. Feed it colourful vegetables, lean cuts of meat. Offer it to a lover, for stroking and praise. Moisturize the soft moon face, floss the teeth. Clip fingernails, their imperceptible grace.

March 21, 2018
Praise

J— worships birch trees. L— the soft fur of a Cockapoo. M— the creamy yellow of macaroni and cheese. Praise. Today, the plumber delivers me from suds: his earring, his beautiful face.

March 22, 2018
Hearts

She shakes in the vet's arms. Her heart a kind of alarm clock. I come home with her pink collar and leash, tags that say "Lichee."

Our umbilical cord is torn.

I clean, discard. How empty the home. There is no evidence of dog now, or the echo of a bark. Only a paw print on the damp soil of my heart.

March 24, 2018
Meds

I have a grief-headache behind my eyes, despite aspirin and cups of herbal tea. Am at the Scottish Bakery on King St., could devour the Easter shortbread and a rhubarb pie. "Are you looking for raisin scones, honey?" the clerk asks a thin old man.

My friend L— arrives with a book: a gift of heartwarming thoughts for a more meaningful life. I read a quote from Margaret Atwood about holding an apple and wanting to cry.

March 25, 2018
Toronto

The shoes I fancy at Nordstrom are $1,000 a pair.

At Saks: a gay couple holds hands. A Chinese gal on her cellphone, gold-tipped runners. Her angular hair and flawless skin. Beauty. Another woman with a bouquet of flowers. A kind of hurt grin.

At Kensington Market, the poets gather. John B. Lee reads from his *This Is How We See The World*. "Ghosts on our breath" I swoon, as I flip through the tome. Marvin Orbach's widow, Gabby, reads from his posthumous book, *Redwing*. Work she found in a filing cabinet; did not know he wrote poems. Honey Novick sings him a Yiddish song. I think Marvin is here in this dark room. A learned spirit: books of verse in his heavy pack. A ghost in librarian's clothes.

March 27, 2018
Frames

I buy new eyeglasses. They are large and burgundy. Made by Ralph Lauren. Drive home in the rain.

My friend L— flies to Dublin today. My mother's people are Irish: Stinson, County Armagh. My great-grandmother was Sarah McQuaid. I love shawls and Celtic brooches, a band called the Pogues, urns of ashes: evidence of ancient souls. Imagine the sound of the sea still in the moons of their hearts, as they wax and wane. The old green waters dragging them home.

March 29, 2018
Indigenous Languages Day, Six Nations Polytechnic

The conference is held in a rustic room: wood floor, stone fireplace and vaulted ceiling. We receive a free t-shirt: words written in Mohawk. I wonder what they mean.

Sarah, our emcee, is working towards her Ph.D. She, her husband and two daughters speak the Cayuga language. Sarah studies Haudenosaunee (or Six Nations Iroquois Confederacy) creation stories like "Sky Woman." She fell through a hole located under the Great Celestial Tree. She was delivered to safety on the back of a sea turtle. A muskrat brought her soil and placed it on the turtle's back. When Sky Woman danced, a land formed creating "Turtle Island" or North America.

Karen, from Six Nations Language Commission, tells us the threat is that their languages will become extinct, they are critically endangered. Only nine people speak Onondaga, for instance.

Another woman, her hair in braids, wears a black hat and large silver turtle around her neck. She teaches Mohawk. Says funding is an issue, including rent. A man from the audience interjects. "They stole our culture, why not hold classes in churches, free of charge," he says.

Lannette drives a motorized scooter to the mic. She teaches the Tuscarora language, closely related to Mohawk. "An 1890 U.S. census determined it was cheaper to educate than to kill us," she says.

Damian from the Seneca program in Tonawanda, New York is Turtle Clan. "One of the most beautiful sounds in the world is to hear our children speaking our languages," he says.

Indeed, when the students from Everlasting Tree School take the stage in print ribbon dresses and smocks and little moccasins, they chant and shake rattles. My heart stirs. Teacher beats a drum and older children join them with a kind of shuffle dance. They receive a holistic, earth-based education, I learn.

Sandy teaches Seneca. She wears a purple ribbon shirt, long black skirt, smart glasses. "I'm not afraid anymore of our language being lost, "she says. She praises her dedicated students, though at one time "teenagers were getting lost, roaming the rez and making poor decisions," she says.

"There are 150 students in the language program in Seneca nation...Let's get over the trauma we've been through and get on."

Later, I read the Haudenosaunee is one of the most ancient cultures in the world. They remember the original instructions of the creators of life on *Etenoha* — Mother Earth. They are the *Ongwhehonwhe* the Real People, the spiritual guardians of this place.

At home, I read "Mohawk Language for Every Day." I walk the river beside a Canada goose. *Kahonk*, I say.

That evening, I wrote a poem that addresses the spiritual and cultural need for a Native Messiah. The narrator is a First Nations woman.

Native Tongue

He is a clear voice
in the wilderness:
river moving on stone
or the last groan
of buffalo.

He is come
with the ache
of fallen tribe;
women abandoned
are carcass and bone.
Children: their rattles.

I am of ear and tongue.
He is word, a suede love.
He speaks of the Creator
before he fell.

His feathers lowly hung.

I listen to his poem.
It is the speech
of fall and rise:
the breath of teepee
at night when
moon drags her belly
and men hold their wives.

March 30, 2018
Good Friday

I rise at dawn after a dreamless sleep. Last night, priests stripped altars, bathed feet. I washed my own: the callused heels, the fallen arches that led to plantar fasciitis and sensible shoes.

All morning, I clean house and think of Jesus: the nails and the tree. I wonder at his palms, the terrible fate of the cross, a lifeline like a tear on a cheek.

March 31, 2018
Holy Water

"It's aqua alta," L— writes from Venice. "High tide: the city floods. Sirens...we walk on platforms outside the church." Here it is raining and windy. The power goes out. I lie in the dark, imagine the bed is a gondola, it moves slowly through the door and into the Speed River. I sing of water, the cold spring quiver. Upstream, the damp dome of night sky: a basilica.

April 1, 2018
Easter Sunday

My mother buys me a large Teddy bear for Easter. His name is Cohen. She writes on a little card that he has magic powers: "Hug him and everything will be just fine," it says. He is a tan colour and has large furry eyebrows. My dog was black and white, her hair quite long when she passed on. I dream of her this morning: a convoluted story of canine kidnapping and return. But when I wake, she is gone.

Today, Jesus is risen. Perhaps he is in his glory, a lovely Shih Tzu at his throne.

April 2, 2018
Sacred and Wild

This poem anticipates the coming of a feminine messiah born of a woman.

Her Blood

My belly a waxing moon:
the ache of lunar-root and bloom.
The women gather
some damp in the gauze
of God again.
Her quiet rhythm.
I, too, am made of blood
and the stains of fair linen
though I dream
of the weight of child:

the Messiah, perhaps.
Her blood sacred and wild.
Another poem about a feminine messiah. This piece predicts her death.

The Wound

Jesus is come again:
a woman great-of-hip
and blood.
The wound a sacrifice
a flower torn open
at the bud.
We worship the red rose.
We nurse it with clean waters
and fair-linen cloth.
We wash the stain
from our anointing hands.

The Lord is fertile and moist.
We will bury her
in the thighs
of the promised land.

In this poem I imagine a feminine messiah born of the moon.

O Holy Night

I am of moon
her great womb
its virgin ache.
I turn in her.
I am a pale orb.
Blood on my temples

and on my heart.

I will come with
the memory of her:
her bones and her milk.
I will preach of her lives:
the phases and their weight.
All that light.

I am daughter
messiah of night.

April 3, 2018
Spring

I pray for the dim day; a dog on bended knees as though her last. She appeals to a god who offers only a bowl of food, a terrible mud.

I pray for the skeletons of trees dreaming of buds like young breasts. The broken bird and the pall of a fallen bush.

I look to the harbingers of good things to come: bulbs opening like the low love of women.

April 4, 2018
Breath

The winds whine and pass through trees like a chorus of slim angels, noisy and who have lost their destiny.

I am sad and so very tired, loss a presence in my gut: absent and here like Jesus.

I am alone-and-not in this beige room littered with poems and books the Lord has written from the ambry of my heart. I am mute really and my tongue a pink stone worn by the steady tide of time and the shallow waters in the dark cave of my mouth.

I am breath, as is the wind, meditating on the mystery of throat.

April 5, 2018
Spirits

April morning, sunny and cold. It is Thursday, I yearn for Sunday church: Jesus on my tongue, though waning like this morning's moon.

I feel the Lord tugging me home: a private practice of tea and spiritual community. My friend J— a Capricorn, passed in January, age 90. A career in educational TV and whimsical poetry. MK— an artist lingered with stroke. I attended a Mass for her on a winter morning, wore my muskrat coat. Her spirit was frail and fingered a rosary, it was blue and hung heavy in her little hands. My father might raise his voice in anger or crawl my wooden floor, tears on his Taurus lips. I look for you, too C—, who came to me in dream this morning. Cautious of *your* father: Lucifer in old leather. His tongue was forked, and his words snaked my heart, squeezed my shallow breath.

April 6, 2018
Women

I wake to snow. The spine of the river shivers.

Exercise class is cancelled, the women gather for coffee instead. Speak of local housing and construction, gardening: hauling new earth in wheelbarrows, waiting for the grass to green before they rake. Wind this afternoon and rain.

I am quiet, an active contemplative. One sensible shoe in the spirit world like an ex-communicated nun. I limp through the simple streets of Preston. *The Lord is come again,* I whisper to myself. *She bears the weight of breasts. And her menses flows like a slow tributary from a greater source.*

April 7, 2018
Pythia

My tongue is scarred with word like Pythia's. She was high priestess at Oracle of Delphi, once navel of the world. My mouth echoes as cave.

But I lie down in a cool comforter and dream I am mute, my hands twitching birds choke with song. Perhaps they are mad with spirit too.

But when I imagine you rest beside me, C— the bed creaks like a Greek fisherman's boat. We prophesy in the language of shades.

April 8, 2018
Voices

Two men argue beyond my window, 4 a.m. The fat guy with a beard pounds on the building door and then is gone. I imagine his belly is deep with beer, that he lifted mugs of yellow ale to his furry lip across the road at the Argyle Arms; sang a little karaoke perhaps.

Does his mother raise her voice in the early morn of Sundays too?

Me, I simply breathe, an apparition in the glass. A Sabbath moment of calm before I begin to dress for breakfast with my friend S— who is troubled by schizophrenia: "The voices scream," she says. Gods in their cups again?

April 9, 2018
Melville Café

She sips hot tea, stares into an herbal brew, drinks as though an elixir. My friend N— is down with depression. Her mind, once a brilliant sun, has set low on the horizon and perhaps will not rise again. But she stumbles in the April snow singing a simple hymn. For she believes in the rapture. She imagines, I think, Christ might lay his wide hands upon her head, and the sickness will rise like steam from her cup: that skull and its liquid.

April 10, 2018
Ghosts

Gulls gather around me like nuns bowing their heads. Spirits move as brides, their hair great with gauze. The wedding gown I never wore also haunts — like a spectre in a closet.

April 10, 2018
Brides

In the dim light of this new morning, I recall the wedding gowns my eccentric friend McK— hung from trees, as though haunted brides of the forest. But I stored my simple dress and veil, an intricate cobweb, in the thicket of my closet. Mailed the ring back to you B— in a paper fold. Wrote poems: "my heart wrapped in gauze," "bruised inside its lace," "something blue."

Today, the physician. Perhaps she will listen to my soft murmur: the old ghost of unspoken vows quivering inside the dense interior of my chest. For I am as Ursuline nun lost in the woods, appealing to pagans and the bones of Christians.

April 11, 2018
Probus Women's Club

Damp and cold again, though E— tells us it is perfect weather for apples. I imagine an autumn day, the fruit rouging on its branches, bearing the weight of spring and the light of sun, like my heart.

M— wears a heavy cross at her neck. Her husband is dying slowly of cancer: a tumour like a bruised *pomme*.

We sing "O Canada." Then observe a minute of silence for the lads and others in Humboldt, Saskatchewan who lost their young lives or were injured. A hockey stick propped against the podium looks like a crutch.

I imagine the parents lying limp like stalks of spring wheat on the prairie. Perhaps the land is fallow this season and so they will not stand rooted and bloom in the wind or in the irony of rain.

April 12, 2018
The Y

The doctor prescribes an iron supplement and a daily brisk walk for my fatigue. Yesterday, I hoofed it down the street to the Surplus Store in the sleet. Today, I join my walking group at the Y and circle the track in my new Nikes. In warmer months, we hike the bush behind the facility. The forest floor is bony with roots, as though ancients have risen from graves. I step cautiously over their remains.

One hiker is heavily tattooed: a green serpent falls from her limbs, as though from a thin tree. Another holds an old toothpick between his lips like a dog with a little bone.

I am shy: my tongue lies like a small fish in a dry pool. But when we reach the forest of dead trees, I want to fall to my knees on a prayer rug of needles like a martyr or fool.

April 13, 2018
Bay Days

Freezing rain tomorrow. The sun a white flag? And so, my mother and I trek to the Hudson's Bay Co. today like coureurs des bois. I recall Henry Hudson sailing an arctic passage in his ship, dreaming maybe beneath a moon soft as suede of the forts he would found at several river mouths. I picture First Nation trappers bearing furs in their slim boats, trading them for glass beads and cloth for their women. I fear muskets and rifles, the striped wool blankets they cradled around them.

April 14, 2018
Sack

Ice pellets pock my face. I walk to the corner store for bread and milk. Check my lottery ticket: *non cadeau*. A dog whines from a car. I imagine a time when I was a woman in an early life, wrapped in skins, bags of fur tied around my feet. My companion a skinny coyote. The thighs of the river quivered.

A neighbour passes me bearing a box of Timbits and a tray of coffee. Her hood a wolf's cowl. She does not greet or offer a hot drink, for I am a lone migrant of a fallen tribe, hugging a sack of meagre provisions.

April 15, 2018
Louis

I imagine D— again, a swarthy French man I met in Paris. On an overcast day, at the Chateau of Versailles he reached for my clammy hand. He did not speak English. And I wondered whether Louis XIV, the Sun King, appeared suddenly as a shaft of light in the museum: I saw dust mites rise like fleas from a powdered wig. Was it he who spoke in a simple tongue: *non* — for it broke from my warm mouth as though *le soleil*. And for a time, the amorous man flip flopped away in his cheap rubber sandals, and I stood royal in my high heels, radiating from the palace.

April 21, 2018
Buffalograss

I imagine my father's stone home, a heritage house built in the late 1880s, south of Galt. He tells me, "Just hose it down, it will come up pink in the sun."

He is not well, dons a pair of rubber hip waders and almost drowns in the pond.

Later, we lie in the grass. He wears a white undershirt. It is dirty in places and tight. I see the imprint of moles.

We slip into the cabin at the edge of the water. My childhood is lying here, broken and dirty. Stashed under the sink, in drawers, on the floor. I cough as I leave.

We make our way to the back of the stone home — the old carriage house. He spins a silver dial until it opens. He leads me inside the darkness. We reach some wooden steps to a loft. There's no banister. I lean to the left, lean for my life. But he hits the trapdoor with his head and reaches his hand into sunlight.

We climb the hill where his white Buick waits like a big bird on the grass. We duck into trees. Dodge limbs and insects. I'm wearing his green rubber boots. They feel obscene in my bare feet. I walk backwards and wince. I tell him, "These trees are dead and dangerous." He says, Nothing's dead here."

But we walk the highway by the river, and there's a turtle in the dirt. Its shell is cracked, and the meat is open and red like a mouth. I am weepy. My father looks towards a stretch of green land. "That's buffalograss," he says. It's long and fine as hair. I want to comb my fingers through it. "An endangered species."

April 23, 2018
Evensong

Today another royal baby was born to Duchess Kate Middleton and Prince William, a little boy. Only hours later, they stood on the steps of the hospital. Kate wore a pretty, red dress with a white collar and held her new child wrapped in a knitted blanket; William smiled beside them.

Soon, Meghan Markle and Prince Harry will wed in St. George's Chapel at Windsor Castle. You, Father W—, were the chaplain there for a time. We were friends at Trinity College, University of Toronto. How you taught me to sing Evensong. You, with your perfect pitch, did not wince at my shy delivery of "O Lord, I call to you; come to me quickly..." You played the little organ in the Mary Chapel, and I lifted my spirit to the vesper light, singing, "Hear my voice when I cry to you," and I set a prayer before the Lord. It rose like incense and was gone like the sun that night.

April 24, 2018
Madness

Yesterday, a young man drove a van onto the sidewalk at Yonge and Finch in Toronto, killing 10 people, mostly women. Today, a distraught guy balances on the roof of the Cambridge Mill, a renovated restaurant in Galt. The nearby bridge is closed. I pass a fire truck and an ambulance.

Grand River is grey.

At Melville Café, the Bee Gees sing "Stayin' Alive." I am alone sipping my vanilla crème. It is Pizza Madness Tuesday. Ricky Martin sings "Livin' la Vida Loca." Last night, I dreamed of a woman with a bruised eye.

Outside, my car trembles. On CBC Radio, a First Nations professor speaks of new medicines.

At Trinity Anglican, my mother and other women read from dogeared cue cards. In Jesus' name they pray.

April 26, 2018
Canes

I praise the light like my cousins who have lost most sight. I think of them often: white sticks tapping their Morse code, waking our ancestors and their gods.

April 29, 2018
Full Moon

Her pale mask. How it fits against her skin to conceal, perhaps the blisters of fire, or the scars of a love turned violent or mad. I think, too, of my father in his black balaclava in the brisk Canadian air. A wool hood, and beneath he rouged with rash as I do, even the scalp beneath our wild dark hair.

Tonight, the Lord. His face cream a thick blue. But in the morn, I imagine His skin is pale and clear as a white rose petal damp with dew.

For I prayed he'd heal the worry lines and crow's feet of His early days, when I was a primitive woman learning to bathe: washing my long, lean body, my hands and face. Nourishing them with mud.

Though green veins remained and the runes of my palms too: the fine maps designed by God. His plan for my days when my father hunted, and I wiped the blood from his tired face.

April 30, 2018
Father's Feet

They were size 10 triple E, perspired profusely (as did his hands), and so he wore silk socks designed for a gentleman. They were fine and dear, my mother laundered them with care. His shoes she wiped with a rag and rubbed with a thick black polish made by Kiwi. My father often rose late. My mother made his twin bed and wiped the spit from his sink. She bent low like a disciple and tied the narrow laces of his Oxfords in small tight bows.

At the end of the day, it was my job to loosen those knots and slip the shoes from his fat feet. The socks were damp and sour. I tossed them down our laundry chute.

My father slept odd hours. His soles protruded from his eiderdown. It was cool on his body and a shade of soft blue. His heels were thick and callused. A flat mole on the ball of his left foot like a tattoo. I have one too. It is brown but round like the moon. I hide it inside a boot.

May 2, 2018
Mute

At age 30, my tongue was a broken clapper in the bell of my mouth. Mummed by a heart so quiet, it spoke only in the language of the Lord: nuances of need and moan and the song of blood as it knelt in silent rooms like a nun. Yes, I spoke only in prayer and in the grace of small movement. Awkward liturgy, indeed. For I was minister to an inner girl who could not hold a tune or the faith of the ages. She was prostrate at the altar of her father mumbling a senseless creed.

May 3, 2018
Langdon Hall

"The poetry of earth is never dead," wrote John Keats. Spring is slow this season, but the meandering road into stately Langdon Hall, in rural Galt, is punctuated with small daffodils and pansies and exclamation points of yellow forsythia. Today, rain falls in the Carolinian Forest as though the Lord composes in anapest.

Inside the elegant inn, my mother and I wait for our table by a large fireplace. I notice apples in a hand-painted bowl.

We lunch in the gracious turn-of-the century house built by Eugene Langdon Wilks, the youngest son of Matthew Wilks and his wife Eliza Astor Langdon (great-granddaughter of John Jacob Astor, the immensely wealthy American real estate tycoon and fur trader).

Upstairs, in the Attic Suite, perhaps the Lord writes a poem in a king-size bed. Something about that small goldfish curled like a comma in the pond below or the ellipsis of pearls at my mother's throat.

May 4, 2018
Smoke

My father's hands were stained with Buckinghams. A plume of smoke from the nest of his mouth. I could not breathe in the old white Buick. The scent of tobacco and Vitalis in his hair.

Today is my birthday. I sense him as the candles burn, for their dirty halos quiver in the dim.

May 6, 2018
Psalm

I wish you Happy Birthday C—. I imagine your mouth a little conservatory for music. Mine is a quiet chapel for meditation and praise. I lift my tongue this Sunday morning, a psalm for you C— I offer my steadfast love. My heart is an ancient door. I anoint its hinges with holy oil.

May 7, 2018
Beautiful Tune

My little blue car: a ghost in the machine. We crawl along Water St., the magnolia trees in bloom. At home by the Speed, I name a little warbler "Beautiful Tune," though its beak is broken and ugly. Its song buried in the deep mind of God. My Chevy and I are not well today and so I wonder at the passing of this bird, small and dirty. I think for a moment it is a fallen glove. Still damp with winter, maybe.

May 8, 2018
Homily

In my struggles to greet God in the arid landscape of myself, I once travelled to Saskatchewan, to the lean yellow prairie and sat on the banks of a long lick of water called the South Saskatchewan River. There I listened to the steady drum of my heart. I drove long dusty days stopping periodically at Miracle Sites and stony images of Mary. I bathed in the healing waters of Lake Manitou where salt gathers in a frill at the shore. I imagined it like the pool of water in John's Gospel, occasionally stirred by an angel of the Lord.

May 9, 2018
Queen Bee

Today, I attend a lecture on honeybees. The speaker, a veteran beekeeper, lost almost 50% of his hives this spring, due to pesticides, the recent ice storm and 10" of mucky snow.

It is a hazardous occupation. He endures about 10 stings a day.

The speaker sells bees to other beekeepers. Most of them, at this time, are young women aged 25 to 30 who wish to save the bees.

Nurse bees care for baby bees.

I am fascinated by the queen bee, there is one in each hive. She has a smooth stinger with which she kills other queens. She is the mother of all bees. The speaker paints her bright blue. She lays up to 2,000 eggs a day in the spring. She doesn't mate with drones from her own hive, resists inbreeding. There are 15 to 20 male fathers for each mother. It is a female society. The queen is fed royal jelly from the other bees her whole life. It helps her to become a sexually mature female. Royal Jelly is made from the protein in pollen and energy from honey.

Bees and flowers are totally dependent on each other.

After the talk, I purchase a jar of liquid gold; serve hot tea and honey to my old mother.

May 10, 2018
Queen of Pentacles

Once I was a babe drawn from a wound: my mother was small.

A birthmark like a petal beneath my right thumb.

Today, I turn the tarot. I am the Queen of Pentacles, a coin on my lap, a garden at my feet. For my heart is moist and pagan as a spring leaf.

May 11, 2018
Furniture

My father was a travelling salesman, made long treks to northern furniture stores in his big Buick to sell mattresses, lamps, chesterfields...As a girl, I tidied his samples of fabric, gaudy swatches of flock. I often leafed through catalogues of bedroom suites fashioned from Saugeen rock maple or trees harvested from the forests of central Quebec. When the founder of a company called Gerard Ouellet in tiny Daveluyville passed, we attended his Catholic funeral: a French Mass. I wore a brown print dress, sat small in the ribs of the church. Factory workers knelt in pews hewed from wood anointed with lemon oil and rags.

May 13, 2018
Mother's Day

My mother was a display artist and fashion coordinator at Simpsons in Toronto during the 1950s. It was a time when department stores often had big budgets for mannequins and fashion shows; even poodles dyed colours to enhance models in gowns.

I imagine my mother padding the soft lining of the Yonge St. windows in ballet slippers, adjusting a wig. Gathering accessories from jewelry, millenary and glove departments, bearing the weight of couturier gowns over her slim arms. Laughing with fellows who insisted on bangles and packages at Christmas tied with designer ribbon.

Lunch in the Arcadian Court with colleagues Del and Peg, still splendid today in pearls. Smart old women.

May 14, 2018
Saints

Today is Cousin A's— birthday. Her eyes are old moons dimmed by clouds. But she celebrates as though blessed by St. Lucy, patron saint of the blind.

Sometimes at night, I stumble through the shadows and imagine I am with dog pulling me through the darkness. I wave my hand at the god in my small room, step upon his orthopedic shoes.

Cousin has a big laugh and sings wide, though she is slim. I draw myself in as though shivering inside a cardigan.

In my dreams, she drops to her knees before the morning light. The big sun, his cyclops eye.

May 15, 2018
Tobacco

Perhaps my father's soul drifted into the last of the Lord's careful rituals. Was he smoke, journeying on wind toward the graveyard of weather? A place for rain and sun and the skin of sky. A place, too, for the lore of men who drew tobacco into lungs, taut as leather.

May 16, 2018
Grandmothers

In the season when leaves open their palms to light and the morning moon is new, the grandmothers come to roost like anointed birds. They coo me from sleep when the shadows of nervous patients and children who tug on wishbones rise from the graves of my dreams.

The grandmothers, the glint of their wedding rings.

May 17, 2018
Holy Communion

My mother's chest was wrapped in cloth, she could not nurse. As a babe, I cried, and my mouth was a hole lined with warp and weft. Only in dreams, her breast a bowl of milk, an offering. "Given," she said, "for you."

May 18, 2018
Aunt Helen

The tired dreams of the dying. The confessions of the sick. *May the Lord be in thy heart and on thy lips.*

Now you are dust. A wind takes what was. Forgive me, I struggle with the Psalms. Though, *I will lift up mine eyes unto the hills.*

You knew little of the soul, though washed it clean with water. Your bath was the colour of sky when we cast your ashes or prayed for your shadow *that fadeth not away.*

Italicized lines from the *Anglican Book of Common Prayer*

May 19, 2018
Silk

Perhaps there are no bounds to my unconscious. It moves out of my mind like a rain cloud. The weight of its belly a sorrow. It sags in Paris at a circus there, raining on the soft pleats of an accordion. It quivers in Greece over the great blue lap of the Aegean Sea. And in Beijing it shares secrets in the Forbidden City.

May 21, 2018
Witches

In the vision, my hair is the shade of burning bush, but the men do not remove their sandals for me. Instead, they call me witch and say I am made of wood. Even my slender fingers are faggots, they claim. And the grain of my heart...

I have a daughter, and she watches as they tie me to the stake. *Her* hair is the shade of corn silk. She is made of milk and pain. *Her* heart is a tender leaf, all those veins.

The flames lick the dirty toes of my boots. But Lord has mercy and lifts my soul like a cloak from a vestry.

I feast with Jesus. *His* hair, too, long, the shade of blood.

May 21, 2018
Virgin of El Rocio

This weekend, roughly 1,000,000 people made an annual religious pilgrimage to the 13th century statue of the Virgin of El Rocio (Virgin of the Dew, or literally Lady of the Flowing Water) in the countryside of Almonte, Spain. They journeyed on foot, on horseback and in gypsy-style covered wagons adorned with flowers, pulled by oxen who wore bells around their necks. Others travelled in large trailers pulled by tractors or in big white caravans complete with air conditioning and running water. They sang flamenco-style songs about the pilgrimage as they went and again at night around campfires where they cooked, ate, drank wine and played instruments. There were also outdoor Masses, horse races and competitions between members of brotherhoods or *hermandades*, organized groups who travelled together.

To reach the shrine, pilgrims crossed a large, protected park full of rare wildlife, including the famous lynx wild boar and many water birds such as flamingos and storks.

But the destination was the shrine, itself — located at the Hermitage of El Rocio, the location where Mary was said to appear to a hunter and his barking dog atop a tree trunk. There, a small wooden statue of the Virgin and Child dressed in a Baroque style of brocading is venerated. Her eyes look downward toward Jesus. On the back of the sculpture are the words "Our Lady of Remedies," believed to be the original name, though she is popularly known as "the Virgin of the Holy Spirit or the *Blanca Paloma* (the White Dove)."

El Rocio is one of the most popular locations of religious expression today. Here, in Cambridge, Ontario I sit by the Speed River, imagine I am a devotee, my hair gathered in flowers, crossing the Quema River in the province of Seville, southern Spain, en route to the Virgin — come hell or high water.

May 22, 2018
Fish

Age 16, Jamaica, my tender body. Mom her salve. But my heart an orchid bloomed in light. Later, the moon moored on the horizon, a forth and rock. Its sails luffing. Time a stain on the shore: tide its rhythm. One night, my mind was a cast pole: dreams hooked and bleeding. The ocean contracted, her great hips pushed. She delivered God. His gills torn. But soft body, still damp and breathing.

May 23, 2018
Scar Tissue

The surgeon, his French hands moved like a tailor. The scalpel tore the cloth of my face. He stitched as though embroidery, little knots. Blood bloomed: a ribbon of lace.

I anointed it with balm, a soft cloth. I changed the dressing: gauze, a stain.

My scar is a half moon. It rises from the horizon of my face. The memory of a cyst, a bulb pulsing in the dark.

Scar raised like Braille, a word for your touch C— It says "Praise."

May 24, 2018
Krishna Temple

I once wandered a Krishna Temple like a lost soul. Guru's shoes were large and cast in gold. A fellow tossed flowers before his heavy soles. He wore saffron and sandals. His head was shaved. He danced and beat a drum, chanted to the goddess Lakshmi. Candle wicks bowed as he passed.

My old soul blinked black eyes: I was a brown woman again. My sari was yellow. My hands smelled of curry and sacred cow. My mind was a muddy river and my heart a beaten stone.

Fellow moved like monkey god through the temple. I rested in the basement, ate creamed vegetables. Prayed to Ganesh, his elephant god, to bear my weight, carry me home.

May 25, 2018
Visions

At Coffee Culture in Galt, I order a citrus-breeze iced tea. It is red and tastes nice. I am waiting for car repairs: ball bearings in the right front tire of my little blue car. There are pretty orange flowers in a white pot on the marble table where I sit. Outside, a man walks a tan-coloured dog. Here, Diana Krall sings. But Galt is tough. I know there are drugs in the white building across the street.

You live in Montreal D— where I attended university. Tonight, perhaps your lovely daughter dances at l'école de ballet. Your little girl is a sylph. You will wait with other parents, sway to Debussy or Pachelbel.

Here, a fellow whose fingers are stained with nicotine. Outside, a pregnant woman also smokes, and a small lady wears a strange purple hat.

D— I recall your almond eyes: the large cross on the mountain, the Musée des Beaux Arts, Moe's Diner on de Maisonneuve where we parted; my student apartment on Lambert Closse where I dreamed of you and your beautiful bicycle, a champagne-coloured Marinoni. You balanced with Libra grace, pedalled away, me on foot limped up the Main.

But today, my Birkenstocks and tonight new dreams.

May 26, 2018
Poverty

My friend S— who suffers from schizophrenia waits for her disability relief cheque. Perhaps the spirits have advised her to squander her last few coins. I will offer her alms, a lift to the food bank in Galt where I worked for a time, bagging groceries for the unemployed and sick. I recall a blind man and his woman. How she described the tins of soup we offered him; the Chef Boyardee. A lame gal drove her scooter into the vestibule. It was wet with rain. She was large and smelled of body odour.

Once, in Divinity school, I accepted meal tickets from kind students who knew my handbag was as light as the Holy Spirit. I dined then in Strachan Hall among the black-cloaked scholars and clergy in their stiff collars. Later, Father H— offered me a $100 bill. I held my hands as though taking Communion. He spoke in French. I didn't understand.

May 29, 2018
Depression

I am worried Doug Ford will be elected premier of Ontario and reduce public health care and eliminate rent control. I am called, as a result, to think of my grandparents in Kitchener during the Depression era. Family members lost their jobs and homes and so my grandfather, a strong man with a magnanimous heart, invited them to live with my grandmother and him and their four children, my father the youngest. Some of these relatives had been well-to-do and brought servants with them. They, too, lived in the two-storey red brick house on Queen St. N. There was only one bathroom and limited sleeping space. My father slept with his brother and a maid in a bed in the attic. My father was sensitive, high strung and psychic. His gift worked like a satellite dish, rotating and transmitting information to his young mind about those stuffed inside the small home of a travelling furniture salesman. There was mental illness in the house, and I imagine my father read the fall and decline of his relatives' minds. Lithium and other medicines were not yet available to treat such disorders and so they suffered the depression.

May 30, 2018
Theology

Once I loved a man who was not good to me. I moved down the street, but in the evenings paced the river like a widow by the sea. My heart a wild and broken watch on a chain. It swung like a manic depressive who had lost her jar of lithium. The man lived on the water's edge where he wrote of God and sang songs of freedom and possibility. He was a scholar. I am a writer who waxes poetic on what is torn. Today, it is my spirit. Its fabric luffs like a sail on a little boat moored in the mud.

May 31, 2018
Poets

It is humid today, my hair hangs in tight ringlets. The smell of fresh-mown grass blows through the window.

Yesterday, I watched a video online of a poet I used to know. He is tall and very thin and has grown a scruffy beard. His hair is short and receding. I remember it long and in curls. I last heard from him 20 years ago when I lived in the cold rooms of my father's stone home. I wrote him a note on small pieces of paper in my girlish handwriting. He did not respond, or share his poems of mother, her small breasts, their cysts.

Another poet has grown stout and grey. His hair hangs in fuzzy dreadlocks. He, too, has given me the boot.

I was bullied as a child and recall the stare of W— who was eventually expelled from our suburban high school. Still, she led the girls away from me like a herd of slow bovine. W— pale and poor, I recall her unkempt mane.

But I have met writers in Cambridge who are kind and embrace me, even promote my eccentric little books. How lovely is E—? Last night her hair in a top knot, she read to us her tale of poppies blooming.

June 1, 2018
Clown and Contortionist

The summer I made sardine sandwiches, I imagined your hands A— opening the can of Billionaires I sent you: the taste of dirt and fish on your fingers.

August was so hot; I stayed up all night and in the late morning went to the Atwater Library in Montreal to use their Chinese fortune books, my future was a fistful of pennies, one of them green.

I watched for the mailman, the one with the stiff waxed moustache, the confident knock. When your gifts wouldn't fit through my slot, he always greeted me with a "*Bonjour.*"

A summer tree planter, you sent me a rock once from MacBride. Said you thought it looked like Oriental sculpture. It came wrapped in a hotel towel, and you included postcards from that northern BC town. Shots of an empty street, a few pickup trucks. A photo of the hospital there. It was a wide, grey building, corrugated like a factory.

I collected your letters and once showed my street-vendor friend your handwriting. We stood and talked by the flea market in Old Montreal as she clutched a bag of candy floss she'd bought her boyfriend. I told her you were wild, like Shakespeare's unaccommodated man. That you had a tattoo of a red dragon on your arm and that you told me it was the nicest one they had in the Vancouver parlour where you sat for hours, the needle buzzing.

Once I went to the market in Saint-Henri. All afternoon I sat watching the fruit vendors, the accordion player, the woman who sold fishing rods. She asked me in French whether I wanted one. I shook my head but stood there as a boy hauled a trout out of the shallow pond into a metal pail. The fish leapt onto the cement. It splashed a little water onto my sandals. I remember the way its bleeding gill looked, and a few weeks later I used the image in a poem. I want you to know I was there that Saturday because I thought we were both carny. That you, with your big hair and love of the colour yellow were a kind of clown. And me, I was a contortionist.

You gave me so many presents that I took the hurts too. I found beauty in the long stick you gave me in Banff for hiking, the box of little stones, the Mexican amulet, the rough sketches of Honest Omar, the big dog Conan and of you hanging from a cliff, a sack of baby trees at each hip.

And once you left me a bouquet of flowers: lilies and orchids and iris. Propped at the base of the vase, three Peruvian burial dolls, one clutching a child. They were burlap, held together by big red stitches, and as I touched them I found a long black hair in the weave of the cloth. Perhaps a woman in the sun had made these little ones. I like to think she looked like the card you later sent of a Chilean girl, big circles of red rouge on her cheeks and a smudge of eyeshadow somewhere it didn't belong. Was it her forehead?

You talked about the train we would take to Toronto, how you wanted to stay with my mother in the suburbs, drink her civilized tea. We would visit the big zoo — the strange birds and animals. I remember months before in Banff watching that beaver sharpen his teeth and the elk drink at the river, how I said his new antlers looked like pussy willows.

Do you remember the walk we took at dusk, how the trees seemed strung together by a kind of spider web? It was prehistoric to me, and the creatures that flew over the water made sounds I had never heard, like boomerangs perhaps. You said you could feel my soul in that place. And I wanted to believe that I once walked barefoot, knew about flint and bats.

I made animal sounds as we took the switchbacks, as I tripped over stone and root. When the trail ended, we gathered twigs and branches and made fire. I told you I was in pain. Every so often something howled. You said it was a wolf.

I thought you would respect me. But when you came to Montreal and stayed in my little apartment, I will never forgive the punch you threw. When I left to do laundry, you tunneled through my papers like a hungry termite. Read the poems I wrote as a 17-year-old, still smarting from Suzie who told me she didn't want me at the disco; me — an underdeveloped teenager tarted up with too much eyeliner, unsteady in heels. You read everything — what I wrote the day I skipped Home Economics and rocked home in my Earth Shoes. All the stupid lines, the highlighted hurts.

I put on my coat, gathered my books, and abandoned my own space. I flew out the door like a shot bird, feathers flying from my down filling. I cried all the way to Guy Street, unabashed. I put my head down on the yellow pages in the phone booth at the corner of de Maisonneuve, angry that they had done away with the sliding door, that the cold was at my back.

When I got to school, I told my friend. I still imagine how he would loosen his wide tie and calmly push his mood ring into your face.

Instead, I tried to forgive, even took a cab in the night to visit you at your friend's flat on the other side of town. You told me it was in NDG, but the driver took me to the east end, the rough part of Montreal I had never seen. We passed prostitutes and dark cars. It was the same feeling I had in the forest months before. I couldn't name the creatures inside the manholes, didn't know what substances were exchanged in vestibules.

You were wearing a suede jacket when you opened the door. You hadn't shaved or washed since you left my apartment. You were more lion than man: your great uncombed mane bigger than ever, the fur on your face, the scent of urine everywhere. And yet you are not Leo, you are Sagittarius, the Centaur. Do you know the myth of your birth, the blood-wedding between the Earth Mother and the Horse's penis? I was foolish to hope that I could ever corral you, that I could muffle the steady beat of your hooves. Do you remember my sign? I am Taurus. How great my longing for earth, my desire for roots and home.

I thought I knew you. I waited every night for your knapsack of words, Orange Crush and Sweet Marie Bar. Remembered the three pairs of socks you wore, the perfect crystal you carried in your Drum tin, the way you whistled when you blew your smoke.

But when I think back, it was in your eyes the first time we met. They were golden, the shade of beer. I didn't know the suicide threats would come, that you might kill. Who would you murder? Someone in the bush — like that man we met climbing a mountain? He came from behind a rock. I thought he was a Sasquatch. Told me he was a writer, though he had to burn his journals. He was up on drug charges: all those mushrooms he'd picked in BC.

It was exciting at first, the way your mind leaned to the other side. You were like a bareback rider, could do tricks without completely falling off the horse. My life was so simple then, I welcomed your circus ways, wondered at how long you could go on juggling and breathing fire without getting burned. Then the note came, the tightrope was so taut, and I looked up to discover I was the net.

One morning, I lay in bed till noon, thinking M— would understand. I wanted to hear again the story of her first husband, how she finally left him, though she had his children, and he threatened to shoot her mother. The phone rang, and it was her. She told me of her new husband, a playwright, of the baby growing in her belly. I relaxed into my pillow as her voice rubbed despair from my muscles and memories: a postcard, a hospital — a wide, grey building, corrugated like a factory.

June 1, 2018
Lords of the Dance

At exercise class, we bounce on large balls to African music, depression in my gut. It does not lift. I drive to Giant Tiger, check my lottery ticket: *non cadeau.*

At home, my mother is in pain. We apply a bag of frozen beans to the site.

I am haunted by images of singles dances I attended at the Newfoundland Club in Galt. Old T—, his quick polka. His grey combover, his shit-eating grin. Michael Jackson singing "P.Y.T. — Pretty Young Thing." S— his offer to take me ten-pin bowling. "Two bucks for the shoes," he said. "My treat. Or chicken wings in Kitchener, 80 cents each."

June 2, 2018
The Rub

At Dollarama, I purchase a cool gel for muscles. When I return home, my mother slathers it on her aching arms and legs. I remember my body as a girl, how it throbbed after ballet class, the tight tendons that never stretched; Mrs. G— correcting me, night after night in her studio above a dry cleaner in Port Credit, for my hips rocked like a little boat. At home, my father shouted about the cost of pointe shoes.

I still hurt, but there is no liniment for a heart that broke. Imagine a balm, the scent of menthol rising from my bra, the telltale stink of the ointment.

June 3, 2018
Choirs

Members of the Cambridge Kiwanis Boys' Choir and Young Men's Chorus wear grey flannels and navy blazers, smart plaid ties. Today, at Avenue Road Baptist, a red-brick church in the woods, they celebrate the choir's 40th anniversary. The boys have sung all over the world, including at St. Paul's Cathedral and Westminster Abbey. I recall auditioning for the school choir in Mississauga, where I was raised. My voice so flat, Miss Darling demanded I sing "Coming 'Round the Mountain" solo. She shook her head, but begrudgingly admitted me into the group.

Today, I imagine a hymn blooms from my red lips. I join the boys in "Christ, We Do All Adore Thee." And outside, a percussion of rain beats in the forest.

June 5, 2018
Alzheimer's

When my father developed Alzheimer's disease, he lay in a bare room in his heritage home. The only decor a fly strip in the old window and a pair of black oxford shoes. At the same time, he suffered from a stress-related disorder in his neck, and when he ventured down from his bedroom he walked like a broken angel. Still, he was wild and when I finally strapped him into my Toyota, he threatened to jump en route to Kitchener. In the psychiatric unit at the hospital there, I settled him into a ward where five other men lay in beds, their chests bare.

Soon, he was moved to a private room and assigned a kind male nurse who brought him Diet Cokes. Next door was a padded cell, and once I peered through the little window in the door at a young Black woman who moved in slow tableaus on the floor.

Dad spent three months in the hospital. I visited often and always brought my little Yorkshire Terrier. Dad and I would drink coffee in the cafeteria or sit in a lounge of disheveled, broken furniture staring at a little television. He would sometimes whisper to me his psychic responses to the other patients. "That boy will never get well," he said of a young Mennonite man. "I don't care for that fellow," he said of a large masculine-looking woman who wore her hair in a brush cut.

When it was time for his release, the staff held a large meeting in the board room to address his future. I brought my dog, and he peed on the floor.

I found Dad a renovated apartment in Waterloo, freshly painted with a balcony that jutted into a forest. He had some care there — a housekeeper and a nurse. He ate meals downstairs in a dining room with tables covered in white-linen tablecloths. But he took to wandering the streets and stopping at taverns for beer.

He eventually died on Valentine's Day in a locked nursing home where he shared a room with a man named Mr. Molson, who lived beyond the blue curtain drawn between them.

The nurses moved my father's body to a private room. His spirit had evacuated, and his face was gaunt. He looked hard and waxed like a turnip. I did not recognize him. I wondered where he had wandered this time.

June 7, 2018
The Broken Body

D's— chin turns up like the toe of a shoe. JM's— teeth protrude. I am spotted with moles my surgeon calls angel kisses. God creates bodies — Siamese twins, harelips. Perhaps we come to this Earth in our imperfection to kneel to Him on bony knees. We bless the Lord and even our words are the fallen beads of a broken rosary. Still, He might gather them as a child gathers stones licked by the tongue of the sea.

June 8, 2018
Prediction

I slept only two hours after Doug Ford was elected Ontario's new premier. My mother paced the kitchen in the night, tip toeing in her clogs, shivering in the light of the refrigerator.

Ford threatens to slice public health care and rent control. I imagine him as a kind of drunk butcher.

This morning, I finger my health card, as though a tarot: duties neglected, suspicion?

June 9, 2018
St. Jacobs

A charming village on the Conestogo River. The old-fashioned broom shop smells sweet. On the street horse-drawn buggies, Mennonite men in hats, their women in bonnets and calico dresses head home to farms. I have come to lunch with a friend I haven't seen in 30 years. She is a social worker now. I find myself telling her my life story. I tear off the little bandages and find the wounds are mostly healed. Scars, of course, but they are pale and fading.

At home, I trace them as though rivers on a map that lead to the tributary that is my heart.

June 11, 2018
Sun

Hot day. I wait for my mother at the doctor's office. She walks with a cane.

I am an old soul, recall the sun in previous lives. Perhaps he requires a wheelchair now as he rolls slowly across the sky.

June 16, 2018
Erasure Poem

A week ago, I was at the Kitchener Public Library for an arts-funding conference and noticed a display on an erasure-poem challenge. An erasure poem is a form of "found art." A poem is created from an existing text. The words that are not included are erased or blotted out, and what remains is the new poem.

In this case, a page from Mary Shelley's 1818 novel *Frankenstein* was free for the taking. This year marks the 200th anniversary of the book, and a large erasure-poem project has been undertaken in Kitchener by the Erasing Frankenstein Collective to celebrate its publication. This group consists of the Walls to Bridges Collective, an organization devoted to offering learning opportunities for incarcerated people, federally imprisoned women at the Grand Valley Institution for Women (Kitchener), as well as students and alumni from the University of New Brunswick. Shelley's novel was the basis of a project that focused on issues of monstrosity, women's writing and various forms of imprisonment. It also offered an opportunity to consider the exclusion of incarcerated voices in publishing and literary circles. Because the novel is often considered a warning against playing God, Shelley also developed themes of justice and imprisonment, which are relevant to the members of the collective.

Participants worked together to produce the first adaptation of *Frankenstein* into a book-length erasure poem, and in doing so highlighted marginal voices, themes and figures (including nearly-forgotten female characters), bringing them into the foreground. The outcome, they say, "will be an enriched public discourse through an open-ended discussion about incarcerated voices in our culture and communities. This activity aims to question public perspectives on incarceration and to acknowledge if not erase the challenges presented by reintegration of the formerly imprisoned into society." The collective hopes "to build and strengthen relations among incarcerated women, students, scholars, writers, policymakers, community justice organizations, and members of the general public."

My attempt at an erasure poem based on a page from the novel:

approach, his countenance,
its unearthly ugliness too horrible for human eyes.
wretched, miserable beyond all living things,
but blood creation, dear to me.
Oh, Frankenstein.

June 19, 2018
Chemotherapy

Recently, a man told me he read my new book of poems, *Out of Darkness, Light,* while receiving chemotherapy treatment for cancer. I imagine the catheter, a thin soft tube a nurse placed in a blue vein. His fatigue the next day. Perhaps he dreamed of my character Mother Scarlett, a high priestess, who offers healing, anoints with river and moon and rain.

June 20, 2018
Rivers

Today, the president of the Cambridge Writers Collective and her husband shoot a little YouTube video based on my book *Out of Darkness,*

Light. We gather by a river and lift our voices, as though the waves call to my character Andrea.

I have lived by rivers for almost 30 years. In Windsor, where I studied religion, I kneeled by the Detroit River and emptied my hurts into her. By the Grand, I envisioned early peoples in canoes, bearing pelts to the outpost. Here, at the Speed, a tree bows from its root. I imagine the water swallows the prayer and digests it in the belly of the earth.

June 21, 2018
Summer Solstice

Today is the Summer Solstice, the longest day of the year with the most generous amount of light. The word "Solstice" comes from the word *sol* or (sun) and *stitium* (to stop), suggesting that the sun appears to stop in the sky at this time. It is a natural day for reflection and for setting goals of transformation. It has been an important astronomical event since ancient times, and as a result, many pagan practices developed. It is still a modern festival of community, sharing and ritual. In Northern Europe, it is the most practiced holiday apart from Christmas. Magic is believed to be most potent on this summer's eve and rituals for future goals for romance and fertility easily attained.

My friends and I usually walk the labyrinth in Galt on the Summer Solstice. "There is a need to come back to nature and be caretakers. Modern spirituality is returning to these ideas. Even in formal traditions people are being environmentally-concerned, Earth-conscious," says my friend B— who studies religion.

But this year, I walk the Speed River alone in my black and white sundress. I appeal to the rays above and to a huge root heaving from the water like the hips of the Goddess.

June 23, 2018
Artemis

My close friend L—, whose lovely eyes are the shade of spring mint, is moving to Port Elgin this week. I think of her as the goddess Artemis pulled by her dogs in woods, by rivers and lakes, relieving disease in young girls and women like me.

She is goddess of the hunt, wild things and the moon. I only imagine I am Aphrodite, goddess of love and myrtle blooms.

June 24, 2018
Greeks

When I worked at *Maclean's* magazine in Toronto, I lived at Oakwood and St. Clair above a Greek family. I had the attic apartment in the house, but no private entrance, so could hear Gus and Metaxia and their three young boys shouting at each other at various times of the day. Sometimes, when I arrived home tired from work, Nick the oldest boy, would slam his bedroom door in my face.

Gus worked at Canada Packers where he carried slabs of meat from one location to another. He was well built and sported a single eyebrow. Metaxia often smiled at me, but in the two years I lived there we never had a conversation. From what I could tell, she cleaned most of the day, though their flat was as small as mine.

Once, my father came to visit and we argued as loudly as Gus and his family. He packed his soft, leather suitcase, and I watched then from the window as he limped across the street to his Buick and drove away. I retired to my white-iron bed, drifted to sleep and dreamed of Odysseus and the Trojan War. How he angered the gods, was blown off course.

June 26, 2018
Burnt Offering

This morning, a venerable Buddhist monk I met when I was conducting interviews for my book *Creeds and Remedies: The Feminine and Religion in Waterloo Region* telephoned. He calls every few months to ask how I am doing. Once I said I wasn't feeling well, and he said he would pray for me.

His temple is in the Village of Blair, a short distance from my apartment. He shaves his head and wears a burnt-orange robe, chants in the language of Lao. He is a holy man. One day I will ask him to clear bad karma from my past lives and rid me of spirits who haunt. He might burn a piece of paper with names of the dead. I imagine my large juvenile script, smoke rising from the monk's steady hand.

June 27, 2018
Linens

Depression turns in my gut like a washing machine. I am wrung out. It is a dull, damp day. I woke at 4:00 a.m. and thought of a priest I once loved. He was defrocked for seducing young men, plying them with top positions in the Church and perhaps above. How he memorized the history of public prayer, the poetry we offer to the Lord: the liturgy.

Later, I dream "O Lamb of God, / That takest away the sin..." while women of the altar guild wash stained linens.

June 27, 2018
Chinese Mood

I recall other lives and remember that depression was treated differently in early China. Patients were brought to a kind of spa where they were swathed with cloths and herbs. Priests and physicians attempted to lift their spirits with natural remedies and philosophies. Family and friends visited the mentally ill and offered prayers, intercessions and alms. They were regarded as people to be nursed and presented to gods. I imagine myself lifted to Shen Nung: his spiritual poems. His words: healing salves. My temples anointed with his laugh.

June 28, 2018
Landlady

For a time, I was a landlady. I managed my father's heritage home in the country, south of Galt. When the place wouldn't rent, in desperation I leased it to a couple of rough guys, who agreed not to party. I lived in a flat in the back of the house with my Yorkshire Terrier, Bear.

Each weekend, the lawn was a sea of vehicles, and drunken people staggered over my land. They gathered around a bonfire and stared silently into the flames. Soon, the tall fellow lost his driver's licence for drinking and driving. We argued once, and he said he had a gun. The short guy was mean too and beat his little dog in front of my mother and me on her birthday. He threw the animal into the dirt repeatedly, as though it was a football. Later, they played "Hotel California" full blast at 3 a.m. I hummed along through the stone wall, muttering "hell" in the dim.

June 29, 2018
Troll

Once I drove west to Plattsville where handsome K— rented an old farmhouse and a barn of goats. I crossed a narrow bridge to reach this place and saw a small, furry troll who wore a vibrant shade of lipstick. I think he was asleep, and my black Toyota rose him from the dreamy place trolls drift. He jumped onto my car and balanced like a strange hood ornament. When I cruised by K—, he crossed himself like a monk.

June 30, 2018
Tomatoes

It is the Canada Day weekend and hot as Hades. I went grocery shopping and bought a cart of healthy food. Outside on the balcony, I am growing cherry tomatoes. I rejoice as they ripen in the sun, fall gently into the palm of my hand as I harvest them. Small bombs of light and rain.

July 1, 2018
Prophets

Two blue herons balance on boulders in the Speed River this morning, stretch their wings wide and fly. I am witness to these birds: Lovers? Yin Yang of nature? I imagine ancient prototypes at the Godhead, prophetic yellow beaks open: so much to predict before they hatch and wed.

July 2, 2018
Snake

A dead garter-snake this morning in the garage where I park my car. I assume it is an omen of something dark. I learn it means good health, luxury and abundant wealth. I imagine it sunning by the river, pulling its belly across the lawn. But today, my heart uncoils at the sight of the serpent on the cold cement, offering itself to symbol and rebirth.

July 3, 2018
Hardy

When I was a girl, I imagined a brother. I was an only child and so lonely I sank my sorrow into the curly apricot fur of my poodle, Martha. My brother would defend me against my father's manic rages and explain his shipments of odd merchandise that would arrive at our garage during his high phases: the boxes of live snails, the cartons of saké, the hundred wool dickies...My brother's name would be Hardy, like my grandfather's; his face clenched like a fist. My father would relent to his hit and slide into a soft heap of depression. I imagined us — his son and daughter — a small psych unit, bringing relief to our patient. Hardy would offer a handful of pink pills from a jar, and I would administer the water.

July 4, 2018
Body

My belly, a full moon, will wane and I will feel my spirit dream. Perhaps she will envision the heavy-set girl I was, then the slim woman I will become. The great exhale of bad energy.

July 5, 2018
Tooth Fairies

At the dentist's office in Waterloo, the tooth fairy hangs from the ceiling.

As a child, I grew large buck teeth my parents graciously had fixed. I wore a variety of appliances, bands, braces and headgears. My jaws often ached at night, and my father watched me sleep inside the cage of wire.

July 8, 2018
Factories

When I was young, my father took me to furniture factories in the summer months when I was not in school. It was usually very hot, and I watched men in tank tops upholster chesterfields and armchairs, their Italian skin glistening with sweat. There were often posters of women in bikinis and other skimpy clothes pinned to walls and pillars in the plants. Large bosoms spilled out of their bras like dough. The radio played loud as the men worked, 70's rock and roll. I recall the sound of staple guns, their steady hits; small crosses around meaty necks: hardware of gold.

July 9, 2018
Preventive Measures

Yesterday, I took my mother to a birthday party on Puslinch Lake, a large kettle lake just a short distance from Cambridge. She is a Scorpio and loved the water and boats, canoes and kayaks. We watched water skiers and their trails of white foam and enjoyed a buffet of healthy foods: a huge bowl of salad sprinkled with goat cheese, soft slices of white chicken, Greek yogurt, bananas, clementines and more.

I played with a baby who wore a string of amber beads around his soft neck to help him with the discomfort of teething. His favourite word is "echinacea": a natural remedy for sore throats and colds.

July 10, 2018
Switzer's

My father sold furniture to a small Jewish man named Irving who had a store on Queen St. West in Toronto before the punk shops transformed the culture. Dad usually spoke in a cultivated Yiddish accent to Irving and often landed an order. We then crossed the road to a diner called The Stem for a freshly squeezed lime drink in a tall glass. After, he took me to a delicatessen on Spadina Ave. called Switzer's for a baby-beef sandwich, dill tomato and Vernors ginger ale. The lunch was only complete after we stopped at Baskin-Robbins on the way home to Mississauga. We always ordered an English Toffee ice cream cone. I am quite sure I inherited my father's pallet. Today, I resist small feasts like this, choosing instead fruits and vegetables and lean meats. But still crave the taste of Dad's ethnic treats.

July 11, 2018
Born-Again Soles

According to Wikipedia, "The human foot is a strong and complex mechanical structure containing 26 bones, 33 joints, and more than a 100 muscles, tendons, and ligaments...Due to their position and function, feet are exposed to a variety of potential infections and injuries, including athlete's foot, bunions, ingrown toenails, Morton's neuroma, plantar fasciitis, plantar warts and stress fractures. In addition, there are several genetic disorders that can affect the shape and function of the feet, including a club foot or flat feet."

Yesterday, I went to a wonderful place in Cambridge called BioPed to investigate my heel pain. A beautiful young woman, a perdorthist who was well-along in her pregnancy, analyzed my feet, my gait and my footwear. I learned that my left calf is significantly tighter than the right and is affecting the fascia of that foot. The gal made several recommendations, and I walked to the car in my new insoles, mindful of the miracle that is locomotion.

July 13, 2018
Creatures

I am cat sitting for a neighbour. Tom looks a little like a tiger, and Lulu is black with a white belly. Both have eyes the shade of geranium leaves. The apartment has a panoramic view of the Speed River, which is not appropriately named, for it is often slow and thick with algae. I am on the balcony in a royal blue Adirondack chair. Tom is beside me in the sun. Lulu is shy and has hidden. I have little experience with cats. I still think of my dogs who have passed. Lichee, her sensitive body, allergic to most foods. The frequent trips to the vet. The complicated design of her ears. The meds I purchased to heal her polka-dot skin.

July 16, 2018
Nun

I read a poem called "Aubade with Burning City" by Ocean Vuong: "In the square below: a nun, on fire / runs silently toward / her god —" But perhaps He lifted her spirit to the light before the war began. Planted her roots in His garden so she might flower in His care, while the fire below took her habit and body, veil and sparse hair.

July 18, 2018
Sun

Before the sun was born, perhaps Goddess rested in the dark, tired and forlorn. How many dreams before that light beat like a red heart, and she stirred from her slumber? Blood pulsing through the veins of this world.

July 19, 2018
Queens

Your face is old but blooms like moon, R—. It haunts me in the night. Its powders and its eyes — smudged and blue. A vein in your neck like a little creek. It flows to your heart, a well. I kneel there with a wish, as though coin in my hand: the Queen and her crown.

July 20, 2018
Gifts

In Saskatchewan, I wrote: "What to offer the spirit of the sad prairie child? I fashion a bowl made of the sacrament of earth and rain: Communion of Goddess and cloud."

July 21, 2018
Song

A spirit rests on a hard chair listening to my heart, a music box: the sound of small tunes and cogs. He is paring an apple with a tiny knife. The curls fall like petals. His heart, too, is light, a geranium on its stem, balancing the weight of white.

July 26, 2018
Vigil

Last night, Torontonians held a candlelit vigil for the girls shot and others who were injured on Danforth Ave. on July 22nd, a Sunday evening. The older gal, Reese, was a scholar and planned to attend McMaster University in the fall for nursing. The little girl, Julianna, excelled at synchronized swimming. Hundreds of mourners processed through Greektown to Alexander the Great Parkette to reclaim the neighbourhood. The gunman, 29-year-old Faisal Hussain (who was also killed), suffered from depression and psychosis, even as a child. Reverend Sarah Miller said in her address to the crowd that she "hoped the incident did not stigmatize those with mental health challenges." Many broke down during a rendition of Leonard Cohen's "Hallelujah." The reverend said that "as people of hope we come together as believers in love rather than hate." On television, I focused on the quivering candles and on the CN Tower lit blue and white in support of the Greek neighbourhood. I recall St. Lucy's motto: "Out of Darkness, Light."

July 27, 2018
Country Club

After a round of golf, the men gather in the lounge for a few pats on the back and a couple of beers. They laugh and get louder as the ale drains. One man wears loud shorts (a wild imprint of flames). A plump guy in a tight red sports-shirt jokes about breast implants. Some pay each other winnings from little sacks of money.

A gal from Kitchener plays acoustic guitar and sings: "Beast of Burden," "I Heard it Through the Grapevine," "Back on the Chain Gang..." I identify with her choice of music.

I am a new social member, have come here alone in my old jalopy, nervously parked beside a BMW. I nurse my soda water, eat my salmon, sip my herbal tea. Someone from another table shouts, "What's your handicap?" I think he is talking to me.

July 31, 2018
Ookpik

When my neighbour returned from the Yukon, she presented me with gifts: I cared for her cats while she was gone. One present was wrapped in tissue paper. It was a small candle shaped like an owl. He is "Ookpik," she told me. I was not familiar with this character, so later read a little bit about him.

Ookpik was a legendary bird, a craze for the baby boomers in the 1960s. Ookpik means "snowy owl" or "Arctic owl" in Inuktitut. It was created by an Inuit artist and produced as a symbol of Canada, a souvenir sealskin owl whose large head and big eyes were made from moose hide. The seal from which most of the doll was fashioned, was central to the Inuit way of life. Seals were hunted as a food source, but the other parts of the seal were also used. The seal fur was salvaged for clothing; the fat saved for lamp oil; the bones used as eating utensils and necessary tools.

The first Ookpik was created by 64-year-old Jeannie Snowball in the early 1960s. Snowball worked at the co-operative in Fort Chimo (renamed Kuujjuaq in 1980) in northern Quebec. The story goes that Jeannie found herself in a snowstorm and was famished. An owl landed near her, and she was able to capture and eat it. The owl saved her life. She created the Ookpik doll in gratitude.

Her owl design was selected by the federal government as a Canadian symbol and mascot during the international Philadelphia Trade Fair in

November 1963. The organizers of the Canadian exhibition discovered Jeannie's cute creation in an Inuit art catalogue.

After the fair, Ookpik became so popular among consumers, suppliers of the dolls could not keep up with demand. Companion toys were even created in 1965, including Sikusi, Ookpik's friend, and Mrs. Ookpik, a female version of the owl.

As a result of its popularity, the Ookpik was registered under the Trademarks Act of 1964 and became a symbol of Canada. The Ookpik Advisory Committee protected the Ookpik brand and oversaw the use of the trademark in the creation and sale of books, mainly children's, clothing, comics, songs and more. Portions of the sales revenue went to the co-operative where Ookpik was first created by Jeannie Snowball.

By 1968, Canada's interest in Ookpik waned and revenues fell. Nevertheless, Ookpik had provided an income for some Inuit and made an impact on Canada as a cultural symbol. Ookpik was also reinstated as a national icon at Expo 67. And Ookpik has remained an important image for some. The Northern Alberta Institute of Technology, for instance, still calls its sports teams the "Ooks."

The owl is significant to Inuit culture and spirituality and is featured in many pieces of art. Inuit myths served as a means by which their community was bound by common beliefs. Although different Inuit communities have their own legends about the owl, this revered bird remains a central figure and character in many oral histories and is often regarded as a source of guidance, wisdom and assistance. Some Inuit believe one of the owl's duties is to collect the spirits of the dead and shepherd them to the after world before the rising of the sun.

August 2, 2018
Blood

I am waiting for a blood test at a LifeLabs in Galt. It is 9:00 a.m. and the place is packed. A woman slumps into a man's shoulder. He wears a t-shirt with a bulldog on the front. A baby rubs his eye and screams, "Go away, Mommy!" A man in white socks and black shoes thinks the boy is funny.

I wonder what I might have in common with this roomful of people. Blood? That red fluid that makes an amazing journey through our bodies?

A woman approaches the desk, says she feels faint, her sugar is low. I worry I also have diabetes like my father and my dog, Bear. How I administered shots and molasses when Bear was flat. It quivered on the spoon.

"See saw," cries the baby. "Where's the bucket? Wee wee...we all fall down."

August 3, 2018
Legion

Friday night karaoke at Legion 121 in Galt. We stand for the national anthem, then friend S— sings Anne Murray's "Somehow You Needed Me." Her voice is rich and deep. She wears a green one-shouldered t-shirt and jeans. She dates the DJ. His mother sits at our table and knits a blanket for the church. I nurse a club soda, read a sign on the wall: "Profane language will not be tolerated at any time." A man named Rollie sings "Humble and Kind." Here comes Kevin: "Quando, Quando, Quando." Bonny sings "Neon Moon." Paul lays down a crutch before he croons.

I study photos of a young Queen Elizabeth and Prince Phillip. They are surreal in the strobe lighting. The women at tables sip drinks. They wear summer t-shirts and capris. Sport short hair dos and glasses. I am dressed in black. A drunk woman with a gaping smile shouts, "You are quiet — too quiet." Tom Jones' "Love Me Tonight" floods the room.

I greet a French man named Marcel. "*Enchantée*," I say. He is from the Gaspé. His wife died 20 days after the diagnosis. I notice he still wears a wedding ring, and there is a wolf on his t-shirt. He takes the stage and sings "Storms Never Last." S— is up again and belts out "Crazy Love." I stare at a plaque that reads "Lest We Forget."

August 6, 2018
Meditation

Tomorrow I will read my poetry at the Art Bar Poetry Series with Marty Gervais and Myna Wallin. It will be held at a café on College St. in Toronto. I feel I should ground myself today before I set off on the bus in the morning. I recall a course I took last summer called Benjue Meditation. It is an integrative method based on Vipassana, a system of insight and wisdom that is 2,500 years old and Theravada Buddhism, the early and original teachings of Buddha. The core of Buddhism is that pain is inevitable and suffering (Dukkha) is optional. This goal is called the End of the Journey. Our teacher was a slim Chinese man, spiritual and kind. He was also an architect and an artist. I found him inspiring: so calm and present in the moment, radiating intrinsic joy.

August 7, 2018
Art Bar

I am early for my reading at the Art Bar Poetry Series, so return to my *alma mater* Trinity College at the University of Toronto. The heat is almost unbearable today, but I decide to sit quietly in the chapel where I trained for a year. I am not alone here, the organist is practicing high-church music. The scent of incense lingers from decades of students swinging thuribles. I once tried, but the thing wouldn't smoke for me.

I sit in this sacred space, though never was a traditional Anglican. Found it difficult, however, to argue with the theology of architecture and hymns; the golden angels above the high altar. Even loved a seminarian, his hair damp at matins. Took Communion from M——. He was a Christian rocker. Called me "Sister," as he lifted the chalice of wine to my pagan lips.

August 8, 2018
Rowell Jackman Hall

I stay at a University of Toronto residence on my little trip. The woman in the room next to me snores loudly all night, and I can hear her through the thin wall. The rain falls in sheets. I sleep fitfully and feel I am not alone in the bed, haunted by spirits who move in and out of me like the light breeze from the ivy-league window.

On the bus home, I look forward to the view of Lake Ontario, but it is camouflaged in fog, a whole body of water is there and not — like a god.

August 9, 2018
First Date

My father drove a white Buick, baby-blue leather seats. He wore a handmade suit and a fedora. He didn't knock at my mother's door, instead threw a stone at the tiny window of the low-rise building he called Sky

Towers. It was in Rosedale, a tony area of Toronto. But my mother lived in a small attic apartment she painted light grey. She worked at Simpsons department store.

She wore a slim black dress and high patent pumps. The car was a convertible, and her short set hair blew a little as they coasted down Yonge St.

At George's Spaghetti House, they each ordered a pile of pasta, half a chicken on top. Dad had a beer, and Mom enjoyed a pot of tea with lemon.

He spoke mostly about money. It made Mom smile. But Dad was a poor tipper; and they ran out of gas before their first kiss.

Still, they were married in September at St. Clements, an Anglican church in the north of the city. Mom wore a Jackie Kennedy gown and veil, satin shoes. It was dusk in the sanctuary, lit by candles. Dad was bathed in shadow and even Mom's pale bouquet was blue.

August 11, 2018
Moment

My father's clammy hand
touches my cheek.
For the moment,
we are well:
not low or high
nor dreaming of horses
bearing our weight
to the water
where we drop
like stones.

For the moment,
we are not blue
but green as breath.
And my father is not fallen
but balanced there
in his gown.
And I am rouged and powdered
almost beautiful in my health.

August 14, 2018
August

I glance at the sun. He is in fun-loving and dramatic Leo: thespian, star of the show.

I drive to the garage in his shadow.

Still, "Mercury is retrograde," writes my astrologer who studies an ephemeris and the mathematics of the skies. During this period, the planets go awry.

Mercury rules automobiles...

My car slowly lowers on the hoist like a bluebird lighting.

Thankfully, "Only a little rust on the rotors," says the mechanic. He has a fringe of strawberry blond hair and a pleasant smile like a priest of old.

August 15, 2018
Downtime

Depression is in my gut like a ghost in the trunk of a tree. I am haunted. She is snagged in my ribcage. Then her breath on my tongue. A spirit like a breeze. Rising and falling. Collapsing like a full moon down with sorrow. Her thin skin and her marrow.

August 16, 2018
The Barefoot Medium

Last night, I attended a talk at my local library. It was part of a series called "My Story." In this case, a woman named Emma Smallbone shared some of her life journey and her evolution as a medium and an empath. She has written a book called *The Barefoot Medium*.

Born in a small town in England, she remembers hallucinating at age 3 with a high fever. At this time, she could see snakes on the floor and a bear in the corner of the room. She believes this illness activated her gift.

Later, she was branded an "emotional child" because as an empath she absorbed other people's emotions. She was an open conduit and even absorbed what spirits were feeling. But she soon developed depression and anxiety and suffered a nervous breakdown when she was 18. Later, she developed postpartum depression. She needed to learn how to work with her gift and protect herself from people she termed "energy vampires."

As a woman who is sensitive to energy, she investigated scientific explanations behind it. She quoted Albert Einstein who said that you cannot create or destroy energy. It remains. Later, I read a little of his theories. Einstein refuted the idea of physicists in the 1920s who argued that quantum mechanics defied belief in energy conservation. But a few years later, scientists learned that although the energy of electrons might fluctuate, the total energy of the electron and its radiation remains constant during its process. Einstein was right, they conceded. Energy is conserved.

Emma talked about the universal energy that runs through everything. She prefers to walk barefoot to absorb the energy of the earth. She connects to animals and other forms of nature. Deer for example are incredibly intuitive; cedar trees will bend when they feel the winter coming, she said. And even small creatures like dragonflies will respond to "a little push from Spirit…Life is full of messages guiding us in the direction of our purpose," she said.

Emma connects with spirits in a variety of locations. "There is crazy energy in hospitals," for example, she said. "People are born and die there…and most of us are not relaxed."

Much of her paid work involves communication with the afterlife. She has given messages to hundreds of people: private groups, one-one-one sessions, public events and Wednesday night services at the First Spiritualist Church of Galt. Her goal is to heal people in need of connection and closure with those they have lost. In doing this and other related activities, she has doubled her income from the years when she was a successful professional photographer.

She has expanded to teaching courses at Conestoga College, including one called "Rituals Without Rules," hosts an online chat group, and runs a metaphysical store where she sells crystals, tarot cards and other spiritual merchandise. She has most recently added Intuitive Guidance Counselling to her skillset, drawing on her almost 25 years as a small-business owner.

"Believe, Ask, Have Gratitude," is her motto. "If you do things for spirits in service, in turn they start to do things for you."

August 18, 2018
Sheets

The rain fell in sheets last night on my way to the Cambridge Centre for the Arts. It was as though my car windshield was blindfolded. I pulled into a Shoppers Drug Mart on Ainslie St. and sat for 10 minutes. Bridges Homeless Shelter on the corner was a shadow.

The play was a local production conceived by Empty Space. I met one of its producers, Gary Kirkham, through Arts Connect Cambridge who funded my book *Out of Darkness, Light* and who also supported Gary's project. The actors were immigrant teenagers who relayed their stories through short exchanges and tableaus. The recurring props were long sheets of white fabric used to symbolize a variety of key concepts or images. One fellow was tied in the cloth while he repeated the ironic line "Everything's fine." In another scene, it was bunched inside a girl's overalls to suggest pregnancy. Later it became a child, a stretch of land, an ocean, an apron, a sling, a wall and a Muslim girl's *hijab*.

As a poet who has explored the significance of cloth in her writing, the versatility and importance of it in this short production really appealed to me. In fact, in reviewing my book *Out of Darkness, Light*, poet Katherine L. Gordon wrote, "Cloths...that heal, console, soften, wrap and comfort, appear throughout the verses in their impactful ancient use."

The kids who made creative use of cloth in the theatre piece ranged in age from 16 to 19 and hailed from a variety of countries: Syria, Dubai, Jordan, Greece, Thailand...They all spoke English. They directed the play and starred in it. Their resilience was celebrated in the final scene: gathered in a bomb shelter, one fellow took up a drum. "Let's be happy and let's dance," they cried. Audience members joined them in moving to the steady beat of the rhythm framed by white drapery that hung around the simple black platform that was the stage. We were players in the drama of their young history.

August 21, 2018
History Lessons

Recently I discovered some notes I made at a lecture I attended in 2015 by Dr. Amy Milne-Smith, an associate professor of history from Wilfrid Laurier University. She spoke at the Kitchener Library on the history of madness, especially during the Victorian age. I thought I would highlight some of the points she made:

- Some Christians identified mental illnesses as forms of divine madness. They considered speaking in tongues holy and a state of enlightenment.

- To the ancient Greeks, madness was a problem of the humours. There were four humours. The melancholic humour was caused, they said, by too much black bile.

- The Enlightenment focused on reason. If a person lacked reason, they were no longer considered a human. These people were treated like abused animals.

- Victorians identified epilepsy as a madness. This age marked the first mass treatment of the mentally ill by the state. It built asylums, but they didn't really help, as officials prescribed mostly opium to treat patients. It was believed to calm manic visions.

- By the 1800s madness was regarded as a disease, a psychological disorder. Doctors studied the brain, the psyche and case histories.

- Quakers challenged the idea that the mentally ill were animals. Man has a divine spark, they said, even if he has lost his mind. The patient is human, and rationality can be coaxed back. They took away constraints (locks, chains, straitjackets…) They put patients in pretty environments and encouraged gardening. They were kind to them.

- By the mid-Victorian era doctors took over asylums. They emphasized the Quaker non-restraint method. Every county in England must have an asylum, they said. They still prescribed opium and the cure rate was low (10%). Syphilis and malnutrition were considered possible causes.

- Artist Richard Dodd (1817-1886) took a 10-month tour abroad. In Egypt, he believed a pipe was speaking to him and was receiving messages from the god Osiris. He had persistent headaches and exhibited odd behaviour. He wanted to kill the pope. He was sent to the Criminal Lunacy Wing of Bedlam Asylum in London, England at age 27. He was encouraged to paint (early occupational therapy). His family sent him brushes etc. But he went from genius to mad. This was considered the danger of an artistic life. The Tate Museum still has his work.

- Charles Darwin's belief in eugenics stressed improving the genetic quality of a population, therefore madness could be prevented by patients not marrying or having children, he said.

- Cold baths were prescribed by the Victorians as a treatment for hysteria.

- Victorian women were institutionalized equally as often as men. Women "did not go gentle into that good night."

August 26, 2018
Gimp

My friend L— is driving to Huntsville today to pick up her teenage daughter from camp where she has been a counsellor this summer. She loved her experience, but I recall my time at Camp T—, also in Huntsville. It was almost 50 years ago, when I was 8. Each girl was given a coloured wire to wear around her neck. Mine was yellow and indicated that I was weak in most of their categories. I felt branded. I spent most of my time alone in the woods at the petting zoo or at Crafty Corners where I made a sloppy ring from plastic lacing called gimp. On our camping trip, it rained, and I woke with my head in a puddle. I was so homesick I didn't eat for four days, lost my ability to swim and wept during quiet time. I was used to bathing every day in a bathtub, there the girls showered once a week in a communal stall. There were also restrictions about the use of toilet paper. I asked to use the telephone, so that I might speak to my mother but was denied this privilege. So, I wrote her a little letter in my childish scrawl. I remember it was on notepaper with a sketch of a horse. Three days later, her wine-coloured Chrysler galloped into the camp. She heaved my trunk full of designer sportswear and a dozen Nancy Drew books into the back-seat, and the exhaust rose behind us like a swarm of blackflies. In the car, I tugged at the cord around my scrawny neck, rubbing the rash there like a condemned witch who wielded her weak magic — a prayer in the woods — and escaped her fate.

August 28, 2018
Rats

Last week, I encountered a dead rat in the grass near the Speed River. I haven't had much experience with rats, though I did have a vision of one in my small apartment on St. Clair Avenue in Toronto, 30 years ago. I also loved Michael Jackson's ode to a rat called "Ben." Today, I researched rat symbolism and discovered that these rodents, which for eight centuries were blamed solely for the spread of the Bubonic Plague (they are now thought to have been hosts for infected fleas), offer many positive meanings. While they are one of the most feared and even despised creatures on the planet, rats have continued to survive (despite being one of the most hunted animals of prey) and so are regarded as resourceful and adaptable, able to withstand harsh environments. They are also considered clever recyclers who scavenge what the rest of the world discards.

In Chinese culture, the rat is the first symbol of the zodiac, and those born in a rat year are said to possess creativity, versatility and intelligence, all qualities associated with the rat. In Asian cultures in general, rats are auspicious symbols of success in business. In Hinduism, Lord Ganesha, who is believed to be the remover of obstacles, rides a rat (a symbol of troubles) to prevent it from disturbing people. There are also several references to rats in the Bible, in Leviticus for example, when the Ancient Hebrews were forbidden to eat rats. In some First Nations traditions, a rat offers protection from diseases and other health issues and is a symbol of survival, as it is believed to have high immunity.

But when a rat comes as one's spirit animal, it is often prepared to help us in our careers: offering creative solutions to issues and directing us toward change. Rat could also be telling us to nurture our family, as it is an animal that cares for its own. What I remember most distinctly about the creature I saw recently was its long tail. Apparently, it is this that allows the rat to have terrific balance, and so it can speak to us about balance in our own lives and whether we have solid footing. When we encounter a rat, it is also seen as a sign that we are about to begin a time of cleansing – either physically, emotionally or spiritually — for rats, surprisingly, are very clean animals and spend hours a day grooming. Those of us who take rat as our spirit animal often resonate with its hardworking and calculating nature.

But lying still in the grass, this brown hump of fur only frightened me. Dead rats may indicate we are overwhelmed by a situation or might need to let go of a relationship. I will meditate on this and the fact that in 1961, France launched a rat into outer space. I imagine its little corpse decaying above terra firma, this great orb that spins our mythology and lore.

August 29, 2018
Spirit of the West

This morning, I discovered an old CD my former boyfriend gave me when I lived in Windsor. It is called "Faithliff" and was recorded by the Canadian band Spirit of the West. I love this alternative Celtic-influenced music, especially their song "And If Venice Is Sinking." I saw a newscast about the band's lead singer and songwriter, Calgary-born John Mann, a few years ago. He is roughly my age but announced he had early-onset Alzheimer's disease in 2014, after a battle with cancer. He said then that he had noticed memory issues dating back to 2001, when he experienced challenges remembering song lyrics and guitar chords during performances. I don't know this man personally but am interested in the spiritual implications of the robber called Alzheimer's. Perhaps the essence of its victims leaves the body prior to decline or death. I hope when John Mann passes, he rises over the Canadian prairie, a free and happy "spirit of the west."

August 30, 2018
Mothers

Cool this morning. Rose early for a doctor's appointment. Dreamed of royalty and wild dogs.

It is 7:30 a.m. I am in Galt. The sun is a fried egg on a white plate.

The gynecologist comes in and out of doors. She is singing.

I observe women great-with-child. One wears a *hijab* and arrives with a jar of urine. The other tells the receptionist she is pregnant with her fifth. "Jesus," says the woman behind the desk. The pregnant woman is busy now with her little girl. She is teaching her to read. The woman is quite far along, her navel protrudes from her thin t-shirt.

I am inclined to care for my old mother, small dogs and a geranium. I grow umbilical cords for them: roots in the soil of my womb. I am that kind of mom.

August 30, 2018
Painkillers

A tattooed man buys a box of Advil at a Little Short Stop in Galt. It says "Canada" on his right cheek. His arms and neck are also inked. A Black man waits for him in a little black car. He lights a cigarette, and they drive away.

I wait for my mother in my Chevy outside Physiotherapy Health & Wellness. Inside, a woman wraps Mom's aching back with heat, touches her with healing hands. Perhaps the tattooed man has taken a tablet by now. I wonder what ails him.

August 31, 2018
Chess

Fresh morning. The leaves on the trees at the Cambridge Centre for the Arts are yellow. Autumn blooms again. Winter will follow with its web of white. I am worried about my mother, pocking the snow with her cane, or scarring it with the slow tires of her walker.

I have a warm coat I like (it is olive green) and high black boots like a pirate might wear. I give thanks for them. Some members of my family are quite wealthy and ride in limousines or drive their Rolls Royce cars to the private schools their children attend. I don't aspire to that. Would like to have another room, one devoted to writing. My mother and I compressed a three-storey house into only a few areas in an apartment. Sold our belongings on Kijiji and at yard sales. One fellow, a lifesaver named Trevor, came with a truck and his little girl. They cleared out what remained in our garage and drove it away. I don't think about those past treasures very often, only a marble chess set made in Italy. My father taught me to play the game on that board. My little hand would tremble over the black-and-white squares attempting to protect my queen — who I often lost. I imagine her as a small woman like my mother. Her crown lying in the snow.

September 1, 2018
Fine Arts

It is Labour Day weekend, I remember preparing for the first day of school at York University in Toronto. I was a Fine Arts major that year. I lived in a residence named for Dr. Norman Bethune (1890-1939), the Canadian doctor who devoted himself to surgical work, teaching and politics in China where he is revered as a saint. He is also remembered for being the first to introduce mobile blood banks to battlefields. He eventually wrote extensively of new surgical instruments and created a body of work that became a central reference for surgeons. And in 1936, he proposed radical reforms to the healthcare system in Canada, arguing for a universal program.

My roommate at Bethune residence was McN—, an artist who hailed from Espanola, Ontario, not far from Sudbury. According to Wikipedia, the name "Espanola" is an anglicized version of the word "Espagnole." The story goes that in the mid 1700s, an Ojibwa tribe raided an area far to the south and brought back a woman who spoke Spanish. She eventually married a First Nations man and taught their children the Spanish language. They lived near the mouth of a river. When coureur des bois and other French travellers came upon the settlement, they heard local Natives speak fragments of Spanish. As a result, they named the river the Spanish River, and the location became known as Espanola.

Espanola has been equated with paper mills throughout its contemporary history, but during World War II, it was a ghost town, and the mill site became a camp for German prisoners of war.

My Espanola roommate was a very-quiet Virgo. I don't think she liked me or most people she met at the university. I was immature and nervous. I studied dance then and thought I might become a critic for newspapers and magazines. McN— was devoted to learning the techniques of the old masters and travelled weekly to a studio in a remote part of Toronto where she apprenticed with a portrait painter. I have since Googled her and her work. She obviously appreciates realism — precise perfection. According, to the Cube Gallery in Ottawa, "Her subject matter ranges from portraiture and still life to landscapes." I am impressed with her technique: the traditional rendering of green apples, sensual pears, the nude bodies of women, though my taste tends towards contemporary and abstract work. I collect Modigliani prints and those of Matisse.

McN— has included a self portrait on her webpage, she has morphed into a beautiful woman, her hair cut in a smart bob. I remember her long brown tresses in 1982, clipped from her forehead in two pink plastic barrettes; her limited wardrobe, likely purchased from a single clothing store in Espanola, home to less than 5,000 people.

I imagine she still wouldn't like me: my hair wild despite grooming; my fruit a little too ripe; my body an imperfect vase.

September 2, 2018
Danish Pastries

My great-grandfather Frederick Johnson emigrated from Denmark when he was 12 and settled on a farm with his family in Stayner, Ontario. He eventually became an itinerant preacher who owned his own bakeshop in Omemee, not far from Peterborough. He was known for his elaborate wedding cakes and loaves of fresh bread. I wonder whether spirits bake in the afterlife. I imagine their pale hands dusty with flour; their wedding cakes — sweet cathedrals. Today, my mother and I speak of her grandpa over open-faced sandwiches at a restaurant called the Danish Place, in the rural community of Crieff. Unfortunately, we are both unhappy here. We find it noisy and uncomfortable. The tea isn't hot, and they have poured something sweet on the smoked salmon. The prices are high and the lunch portions small. I assume my mother's grandfather is disappointed by this. It is the first time I have investigated his cultural cuisine, and I have been left hungry.

September 3, 2018
St. Peter's Abbey, Saskatchewan

It is Labour Day Monday, and I am culling old files. I find a journal written in 1992, when I was 29:

July 24, 1992 — July 30, 1992

"I live in a small apartment in Toronto across from the Budapest Diner...

It is very pleasant up here in the air en route to Saskatoon. I have had a few glasses of white wine. I am in an aisle seat next to two Australians, hippie types. The woman is reading Sartre and the other, a young blond man, a biology text. A couple beside me seems taken with each other. He hasn't slept in 48 hours and is sprawled over the seat — and her. His white sweat socks are exposed....

I am writing from O's— bed. Her dog, Scooter, is beside me. LB—, her mother, is Cree. She gives me two blessed stones. One is perfect, the other is not. She says I must speak to them...We listen to Starhawk, a Wiccan author, lecture at the University. Lots of earthy prairie women...

I am at a Carmel shrine. I am very frightened. I don't want to get out of the car. I look everywhere for a spiritual sign. There is a stone structure and a statue of the Virgin Mary with her little King. I think I would like to smoke my clay pipe here. Someone left flowers in a tobacco tin...My rental car hits a big rock on my descent down the hill.

At St. Peter's Abbey, the trees look like monks. I see pigs in a barn. One has hairs on his chin...I am in the graveyard. I can hear the moan of a train and birds and crickets. It is so nice to get out of that squeaky room. The woman next door to me has bad energy, I think. Her son took her placenta to 'show and tell,' then they buried it in the herb garden.

There is a shrine in the courtyard outside my room. It looks like a bird feeder, though there are figurines inside: the Virgin Mary, two angels, a vase, eight plastic roses and cobwebs. I speak to Father Alfred after Noon Praise. He designs stained-glass windows. He says the definition of life is 'self in motion.' He can say it in Latin, too…A rooster just crowed…The sun feels nice on my legs…The monks wear their street and work clothes during the day: rubber boots and jeans. A Brother in the kitchen has a big seat, he sports dress pants, a shirt and tie and groovy 1960s boots.

Out for an evening drive. The rental car makes a funny sound on the highway. Then it gives out completely on a corner in Humboldt. Jason from the Shell comes by. He is a good-looking teenager. His dad and ma pull up, and Dad gets out to assess the situation. He says "eh" a lot and "shit" when he slaps the mosquitoes from his arms. He thinks there is a hole in the oil pan. Joe Dewchuck arrives with the tow truck. He has buck teeth. He tows her down to the Mohawk.

I think of the men who help me with my damaged car as saintly. I want to write a poem about Joe: 'My car and its blood. Joe Dewchuck lifting it from the scene — a weird pietà.'"

September 3, 2018
Retreat

A journal entry from September 11, 1992, my first week of Divinity school:

"I am at St. Joseph's retreat in Toronto with the Divinity class. It is very clean here. We watch a movie called *Jesus of Montreal*. I sit beside Father S— he breathes heavy. The rash around my neck is much worse. It is the shape of a clerical collar.

Cousin P— was born yesterday. He has a little Band-Aid on his foot.

The wall in my room is peach coloured, and Jesus is hanging there. There is also a watercolour of pansies. There are pansies in vases everywhere.

Sister Bernadette wears a navy polyester suit.

In the car on the way here, we escaped a minor accident with an ambulance. One woman said, "Lord on board." We had Compline this evening: I like a service before bed.

I don't fit in, but there is a calm.

I have an image in my head of the altar at Hart House, U of T. The fair linen breathing in and out like a great lung."

September 3, 2018
Divination

Another entry, a prediction that never came true…

November 10, 1992

"I am upset after Evensong, seems R— isn't interested in me. I have dinner with three supportive Divinity women at Swiss Chalet. Still, I take the subway to Yonge. I walk the wet street until I find a tearoom. It is up a flight of stairs. The comfort of country music. The reader is a Russian woman named Nadia. She says R— and I will likely get married, he has just been busy, is all. I will get pregnant soon: my teacup smells good."

September 5, 2018
Tutor

Today, I am reading more old journals and discover one written in Windsor, where I was a graduate student in religious studies. I worked part-time there as a teaching assistant who marked papers. I was also a tutor for a blind man who was studying religion. He was a refugee from Lebanon who spoke English very well, as he had been raised in an English-speaking blind school run by Christians in the Middle East. He worked as a language translator in medical camps during wartime. He had a wife (an albino woman) and two sons in Lebanon.

My job included reading to him, helping him with essays written on his talking computer and driving him to school. He paid me from his social-assistance cheques and treated me to Lebanese cheese pies. He also gave me free packages of Zoloft, an antidepressant we had both been prescribed. A— had quite an impact on me, and I read now in my diary that I dreamed on April 1, 1996 of "a map under the skin of his back." Perhaps he had international ties, for he eventually announced to me that he was a member of a subgroup of the Palestine Liberation Organization and "hated filthy Jews." He had been "hit in the ear during terrorist warfare," he said and that is why I had to pin a small microphone to my shirt when speaking to him.

I began to pull away. He frightened me and had become flirtatious, saying he wanted to buy me a ring; that I was "terribly beautiful." While I typed on the computer in his very-small bedroom, he often heaved his body up and down on his mattress making it squeak above the din of Arabic news on the radio.

When we finally quarrelled, I left my job with him. We arranged days later to meet on Ouellette Ave. and for him to pay what he owed me for my work. He wore a snug wool toque draped over one eye, loose corduroy pants and an ugly grey winter-coat. He was clinging to the arm of a swarthy-looking man who was holding a wad of cash. "Give it to her," said A— harshly. The man handed it to me and then led the blind man toward the skyline of Detroit.

I saw him again on campus. He was obviously lost. He circled around and around like a dog chasing his tail. I just watched.

September 6, 2018
Holy Man

When I was in my late 20's, I felt a calling to the Church. I hadn't been to a service in over a dozen years but began to have religious dreams of nuns and clergy. I felt drawn to an Anglican parish on St. Clair Ave. in Toronto when I passed by it on the streetcar. It was called St. Michael and All Angels. I decided to attend one Sunday and discovered it was a predominately Black congregation, and the rector was a tall White man, Father E—. He was a dramatic and charismatic priest who knew my father, as they both hailed from Kitchener. I felt comfortable there among the Black women in their hats and bright colours, some of whom had emigrated from islands I had visited — Barbados, Jamaica and Bermuda. I often took notes during sermons, as I thought the Biblical and theological language might lead to new poems.

One Sunday, a visiting priest, originally from Barbados and who taught at Trinity College, University of Toronto, tapped me on the shoulder and said I belonged in Divinity school. Father M— held a Ph.D. from Harvard University and taught pastoral theology at Princeton. He looked like a Black angel — handsome and dapper. I was so overwhelmed by his academic proposition and by him, I agreed.

Shortly after, I attended a poetry conference in Ottawa given by the

League of Canadian Poets. I wasn't feeling very stable there and was haunted by images of this priest and by the sounds of church bells. When I returned to Toronto, I learned that Father M— had died at the altar that Sunday, celebrating the Eucharist. He had a heart attack before the congregation at St. Michael and All Angels, the host in his hand. He was 49, married and had a young daughter.

I was terribly upset, though I hardly knew this man. At his funeral, I wept, as did many of the 600 others who attended. Two bishops officiated during the two-hour service that was marked by extraordinary hymns and solemn prayers. Clergy processed in beautiful vestments.

Father M— "fought for the underbelly of the church," said Father E— during a powerful eulogy.

Apparently, as a Black man he was interested in the hardships many visible minorities endure in Canada and in the Church. He even wrote a report for the Diocese of Toronto that was the basis of a policy statement on multiculturalism. He seriously considered becoming a physician, but his doctoral work focused mainly on development issues in religious conversion.

I am not sure whether I would ever be considered a convert, but I did follow through with a year of Divinity school, despite the loss of this man, who I thought might become a mentor. I was even a taper bearer at a service for him at Trinity College where a soloist sang the spiritual "There Is a Balm in Gilead."

While there, rumours circulated that Father M— had been very unhappy at the school. There were employment issues that affected the whole faculty, especially him. I had challenging times at Trinity College, too. The workload was very heavy, I had intense friendships that didn't last, and I was not well. I also couldn't commit to Anglicanism, despite my love of its liturgy and architecture. And so, I withdrew after my first year. I decided to devote myself to poetry, though was haunted by a spiritual calling that eventually led me to Windsor where I obtained a Master's degree in religious studies, a broader focus that included courses on world religions and new spirituality. But from time to time, I have read the leaflet from Father M's— funeral, the Anglican liturgy that I still find poetic, despite my crisis of faith: "Acknowledge, we pray, a sheep of your own fold, a lamb of your own flock, a sinner of your own redeeming. Receive him into the arms of your mercy, into the blessed rest of everlasting peace, and into the glorious company of the saints in light."

September 7, 2018
Rabbits

Yesterday, while sweeping my porch, I discovered a very-small bunny among some leaves. I tapped my broom, and he hopped. Later, I did a little research into its spiritual significance and learned that in many myths and legends, rabbits, though often considered timid animals, are called upon to supervise shamanic journeys and teach shamans sacred rites, as they are regarded as effective guides between earth, heaven and the underworld. They are navigators of the darkness and so represent seers and psychics and other sensitive people who use their inner light. Some Indigenous groups portray Rabbit as the Great Hare, a hero who created the world and brought humans fire.

But rabbits are a common animal of prey and are victims in the animal kingdom. Symbolically, they may appear at times when we are hunted and need to camouflage ourselves and hide, or conversely when we have not been recognized by our peers. In nature, rabbits live in fear, and so some Native teachings remind us that focusing on what frightens us can manifest that very thing in our lives.

Rabbits have also been regarded as humorous tricksters, for when chased they move in an unpredictable manner, or they retreat. They have keen senses and are clever. They are terrific escape artists, burrowers who in the wild can create deep maze-like caves open at both ends. Carrying a rabbit's foot or totem, then, might bring luck or serendipity.

Rabbits are also linked to seasonal changes of Mother Earth, the freshness of spring, in particular. As vegetarians, their diet, which is light and green, symbolizes health and reminds us of the importance of balance in what we eat. They are also historically associated with the celebration of Easter and its Christian themes of sacrifice, redemption and resurrection. But they are also linked with Ostara, a Germanic fertility goddess who was depicted with the head of a sacred hare. Ostara is connected to the Vernal Equinox. In contemporary times, this hare has been depicted as the Easter Bunny.

Moreover, the rabbit's legendary powers of reproduction (a mother rabbit can produce up to 40 or more babies a year) can suggest various types of fertility and newness of life. These might include starting a family, a garden or even a financial portfolio. For this to happen, it is important to stay still and silent like the brown bunny I saw on my porch. For rabbit symbolizes reflection. If we listen, he can guide us on a retreat within and help us to collect ourselves and even guide us out of a rut. His powers of hearing and vision remind us to utilize our own inherent tools. But his magical ability to hop to heights of over nine feet should help us to herald his spirit of play.

September 11, 2018
9/11

I am at Dr. Beth's with my mother. She has the flu and her right knee and hand are sore. She thinks it's arthritis. There is a pharmacy in the waiting room. A nice-looking man, maybe from the Middle East, seems to be the owner. He wears a pale-blue oxford-cloth shirt. A customer is speaking to him in a foreign tongue. I can hear the click of pills as the pharmacist works. He puts a vial in a paper bag, and the man leaves.

An old woman limps through the door that leads to the doctor's office. Her hair is short, white and fuzzy. She hasn't groomed.

A teenager with a baby arrives. The baby is pulling at magazines. "Please don't," says the young mother.

A man with a week's growth on his face exits the office. I wonder how the doctor could stand to touch him. He looks dirty.

I am so tired. I thought I could work part-time, but my energy tank is low. I am a car running out of gas. My mind chugs and is slow.

A girl waits with a social worker. The girl describes a movie about aliens. "Some aliens are friendly," she says. Now they are studying a quiz that improves social skills.

It is September the 11th, my grandmother's birthday. I remember I lay in a green room in a basement in 2001 when terrorist airplanes passed through twin towers in New York City, and almost 3,000 people were killed. I watched later as the rubble gathered speed like a tumbleweed.

"Clarisse," calls the nurse, and the girl and her worker disappear behind the door. I was looking forward to learning about social skills.

September 14, 2018
Roadkill

Last night, I dreamed I returned to the three-storey building where I used to live in Windsor. I was looking for C— who had been my neighbour. I spoke to my friend SW— who still lived there.

SW— was a creative fellow who attended a variety of 12 step programs, as he had been a heroin addict and a male prostitute. He told me he had AIDS. He often drove to Detroit and bought up Elvis and Marilyn Monroe figures at a discount and sold them for profit by placing ads in the *Windsor Star*. He always had a project on the go. Once he drove to Florida, stopping at times to photograph roadkill.

SW— had regular parties for his friends. There was a small group who would gather for dinner and fun in his apartment, which was decorated in leopard skins. They often made steaming stir fries and would later dye their hair. SW's— boyfriend was a hairdresser. I wanted him to dye mine. One young man had a bad scar. A serial killer blew his arm off with a rifle at a drive thru in Detroit, as he was reaching for a burger through the window of his car. Doctors were able to sew it back on.

Unfortunately, I was never invited to one of SW's— parties, but he did ask me to perform in a film he made about gay fellows in Windsor. I played a nun in a graveyard.

September 15, 2018
Salves

My mother was born two weeks after Black Tuesday, when the stock market crashed in 1929. The Great Depression that followed lasted for 10 years, but her parents and family survived, as they owned general stores and a gas station east of Toronto. They carried essentials that sold despite their customers' financial hardships. My mother and her three siblings worked in the stores. My mother hauled cases of canned goods, stocked shelves, served customers, worked the cash, delivered groceries, ran the post office, lubed cars and pumped gas, regardless of her diminutive stature and young age. I always equate her childhood with Victorian child labour, which was the norm in the 1800s before child protective services.

When I studied creative writing at Concordia University in Montreal, I wrote a book of poetry loosely based on my mother's experiences in the general stores and on the eccentric customers who shopped in them. It was called *A Salve For Every Sore* (Cormorant Books, 1991).

Recently, my mother has suffered arthritic and other pains but has treated herself with rubs and home remedies based, she says, on knowledge gained from the limited drug departments she ran in the family stores. I wrote in my book of a customer I called George Sidney. Marie, the character I based on my mother, measured his shoulders for a Belladonna Back Plaster. "*The pain feels like broken wings,*" he said. He was an unusual fellow who shared his visions of angels with my mother as she served him. I wrote that "They beat their feathered arms, rose / like prayers through the stained ceiling."

In another poem, Bud — a kind of quack who promised his salve was a reliable antiseptic and healer — "digs his pinkie into a white jar / as into an itchy ear." It was "a dime for a little drum of miracle lard."

I have always been interested in what one of my characters, Eliza Jane Davidson, calls "stinks, potions and medications." In fact, my first written effort was a collection of poems fastened with a staple I called "The Flannel Brew." While my mother is not a witch, I admire the simple pharmacy she runs from her little bathroom: the wrinkled tube of Voltaren, the jar of Aspirin, the Tums, the warn blue heating pad. Her homey approach to medicine is based on her childhood work experiences and her father's frugal ways. My grandfather would brew up a pot of ginger tea for a sick stomach, paint a bad tooth with clear nail polish. I wonder what he would prescribe to chase my mood swings away.

September 16, 2018
'Psycho'therapy

Years ago, when I lived with my father in his stone house by the Grand River, I saw a psychiatrist regularly who made the front cover of local newspapers. I found Dr. K— rather cold and unresponsive, but those were the least of his shortcomings. He was fired, stripped of his medical licence and eventually sent to prison for fondling and performing sodomy on young boys in his office at the hospital. He committed these obscene crimes on the very couch where I sat each month.

Another "professional" I saw in Toronto, a psychotherapist who practiced from an upstairs room in her home, encouraged me to sit beside her during sessions on a futon on the floor. On a couple of occasions, she rolled onto me and began viciously wrestling me with all her might. I wasn't sure at the time whether this was a new therapy technique designed to rid me of angst, or whether she wished me harm — or even worse. Luckily, she was an old woman and I, despite the weakness that brought me to her, was able to launch her into the air.

I could have retired my search for a doctor who would rid me of the psychological pain I felt in my gut, chest and throat — a pain I used to imagine was the colour green. But I continued with Taurus tenacity. I found a few sympathetic and healing souls who listened with care and a prescription pad. One friend commented that I "bloomed, as a result." Now I believe the shade of green I imagined was a huge bud, and from it blossomed my true self.

September 17, 2018
Pocket Change

Yesterday, I took my mother to the ballet at the Hamilton Family Theatre in Cambridge. We saw a performance of Coppélia danced by Canada's Ballet Jorgen, based in Toronto, and members of the Hong Kong Ballet. The dancers were top-notch and received a standing ovation. My favourite scene took place in the magician's house inhabited by strange creatures in wonderful costumes: a tweety bird, an electric guitar, a green monster…I prefer modern forms of ballet and dance, and these fantastic toys appealed to my contemporary aesthetic sense and love of dream imagery. I have never choreographed anything to music, though I danced for years and still take a class once a week. I hope to create a kind of dreamscape with words at some point, like Dr. Coppélius did with his dolls in the production yesterday. My challenge is always to translate the weird and unique imagery of night reverie to something universal and archetypal. The famous Swiss psychiatrist Carl Jung attempted this. I analyzed with a Jungian dream therapist intensively for two years in Toronto. I tugged at the lining of my unconscious mind, as though a pocket, and released its loose change and trinkets. All those valuable coins and other little treasures tumbled out of the dark fabric of my pouch quite quickly. I tried to catch them as they fell.

September 18, 2018
Fall Fair

Jesus, his straw hat. His future in a cup of tea: his heart a candy apple, sticky magic seeds.

September 18, 2018
Tenants and Tenets

I moved to Cambridge, Ontario in 1995 after the tenants who were living in my father's heritage stone house set it on fire. Their little boy was playing with matches, and soon the old summer kitchen was ablaze. They managed to escape, but their family cat died. They moved out shortly after, never notifying my father of the accident or the damage, which was significant. My father who was high strung at the best of times was beside himself when he finally heard the news. He spoke to the fire department who said the fire was so great, it was still smoldering the day after they arrived, and they returned with their trucks. My father always had a sentimental attachment to that house. It was built in the late 1800s and set on over eight acres of land across from the Grand River. It featured original pine floors, a stone fireplace and a carriage house.

I moved to the forlorn home from Windsor, where I was a student, to help repair the damage and to build an apartment in the back for myself. I began by washing soot from the floors and from furniture we had stored. Shortly after I began this task, a fellow came to the door and said he was a carpenter and painter and was looking for work. He gave me a fair estimate for the cost of the project, and I hired him. V— was a very-hard working and extremely talented French guy who had been born and raised in Galt. His work was impeccable, and he even knew of a special paint designed to cover smoke damage. He had a Leo flair for the dramatic: he wore his cap on such an angle, it reminded me of a French beret. His moustache and Catholic crucifix suggested his heritage too.

I loved my country flat and lived there for five years. It was unique and arty and offered a view of a big pond on the property, as well as the river. But there were drawbacks: it was cold, as it lacked insulation and was designed to be a cool summer kitchen. And sometimes, I had to share the property with tenants who seemed to resent me. One group wanted me to party, whereas another preached an unusual form of fundamentalist Christianity that involved Hanukkah and Passover, as well as Christmas and Easter. I was either too conservative or too liberal. In either case, I wasn't myself. I was also alarmed one night, when my dog woke me at 3:00 a.m., as there was an issue in the house. I soon detected that the tenants' kitchen was full of smoke; they had left the oven on. The matter was handled by a young man who lived in the basement. The family gave thanks to God for waking him, but never apologized to me or my dog.

September 20, 2018
Pants on Fire

When I was a student at York University in Toronto, I worked part-time at Simpsons in the bargain basement. The department was managed by Mr. D— who was a born-again Christian and who ran our morning staff meetings like old-time revivals. He tended to hire and promote young people from his church. The name of the department was "The Last Stop," which was a pun since it was close to the Queen St. subway station. The clothes, mostly rejects from other floors in Simpsons, were sometimes piled in mountainous heaps, others were rammed onto racks or lay on the floor. They were mostly made of cheap polyester. Once, while patrolling the merchandise, I noticed a pair of purple stretch pants in a corner. They seemed to have combusted and were ablaze. I ran and found one of Mr. D's—disciples and he and I quashed the flames. It could have been a serious situation, as that much polyester in one location might have consumed the floor in fire. I always thought that fabric should have come with a warning sign.

September 21, 2018
Peep Hole

When I lived in Windsor, my neighbour, P— rented an old one-bedroom apartment she painted grey and purple. Her wooden door did not fit properly in the frame, and it made a terrible grinding sound when she opened it. She often woke me up at ungodly hours.

P— had pretty shoulder-length red hair and often wore jeans and plain t-shirts to her job at Dr. Disk, a music store on Ouellette Ave. One day, I noticed through my peep hole that she had cropped her hair and bleached it platinum blonde. She looked like Marilyn Monroe.

She never spoke to me, even when her cats escaped into the hall and our eyes met, though she sometimes appeared at clubs I attended on weekends. She stood at the back of these dark rooms staring at me.

Years later, I Googled her. She had moved to Toronto and started her own sexy underwear and fetish business. She sewed bustiers and rubber dominatrix gear and sold them at trade shows. She also engaged in part-time prostitution with both sexes. There was a photo on the Internet of a woman bound to a wall with various ropes. The caption read, "Tying Up a Client." Once I came across a site where P— had posed stark naked. She had a tattoo of a sun design in the small of her back. I wondered why she had chosen such a bright image, when it seemed to me she had aligned herself with the powers of darkness.

September 21, 2018
Higher Education

In attempt to receive some higher education, I moved to university cities in my younger years that I discovered weren't always safe for a single woman. Windsor, with its proximity to Detroit, attracts people who are sometimes involved in lascivious behaviour. In Montreal, I was robbed. I went home to Toronto for a couple of weeks, and when I returned to my apartment at Atwater and de Maisonneuve a thief had removed my door from its hinges and helped his or herself to some of my 'treasures.' These included a black-and-white television set, a collection of trendy brooches and a sack that read "Laundry Sucks." My beloved janitor, Monsieur Rondeau, was in the hospital during this time, and there was little supervision of the building. He was an old French-Canadian man, whose friends sometimes carried him home after a night of drinking, singing classic folk songs in their mother tongue that woke me from dreams.

After the robbery, I was frightened the thief would return to do me harm and so slept with the lights on. Even Monsieur and his cronies could not relieve me of my anxiety. It was around this time, I created my character named Beauty who was central to my short stories. She was a diffident yet resilient gal who encountered various forms of evil. Someday, I hope she will be featured in a film. I imagine a hauntingly beautiful actress, dressed in vintage clothing. Perhaps the movie will be called "Open Thou Mine Eyes," a line from the Bible, for Beauty was a little naive and shy, her cousin Harvey, a paint and wallpaper salesman, flirtatious with her and doting.

September 22, 2018
The Weight of Wings

Many years after I had graduated from creative writing school in Montreal, I wrote a little book of poetry called *The Weight of Wings* (Trout Lily Press, 1997). It was truly a labour of love. It took 10 years to write, during which I moved several times and received a Master's degree in religious studies. I also suffered a major depression, that brought me quite literally to my knees, and so I wrote some of the poems on the floor of my apartment in Toronto in the west end of the city, near St. Clair and Dufferin.

It was a large one-bedroom that featured hardwood floors and a nice view of Italian gardens. The book, ironically, was set in Saskatchewan and featured a variety of characters who spoke about their spiritual lives, including a convent of nuns called Sisters of the Sacred Heart. None of these people was a traditional believer, still I received a letter from my former thesis director in Montreal after the collection was published who said he didn't like the direction my work was going — that I was using words like "God." While his review of my little book touched a nerve at the time, and we severed ties after that, the book was shortlisted for the Pat Lowther Memorial Award for the best book of poetry written by a woman that year. And so, I continued to write about a variety of religious traditions and theological concepts that interested me. I have developed beliefs, as a result, that draw from a variety of sources and reflect my studies and mystical interests.

"The Weight of Wings" is an apt description of my own literary, psychological and spiritual journey. It has been a bumpy flight, characterized by extreme highs and lows. My wings have been torn and patched several times.

September 23, 2018
Fall Equinox

Last night, at 9:54 p.m. we experienced the fall equinox — the sun was directly in line with the equator. And the season shifted from summer to autumn. There was also a large full moon in Aries. I did not sleep well.

The word equinox literally means "equal night." During the autumnal equinox, most places on Earth will see approximately 12 hours of daylight and 12 hours of night. From now until the winter solstice in December, our hours of daylight will shorten. This is due to the Earth spinning on a tilted axis. This tilt was possibly the result of a gigantic object striking the Earth billions of years ago, causing the North Pole to be positioned toward the sun for half of the year, and the South Pole the other half. The tilt is why we have seasons.

Some people flock to Mexico during the equinoxes — to the pyramid at Chichen Itza on the Yucatan Peninsula. This pyramid was built by the Mayans over a 1,000 years ago. It was designed to cast a shadow at the time of the equinoxes outlining a feathered snake god. As the sun sets on the day of the equinox, the sunlight and shadow reveal the body of the serpent slithering down the pyramid steps.

At Machu Picchu in Peru an ancient stone monument, a solar clock called the "Hitching Post of the Sun," marks the dates of the equinoxes and solstices.

Today in Cambridge, it is warm, and the sun is throbbing in the sky. Some of the leaves on the trees are quivering in a slight breeze. I, myself, am tilting like the Earth on her axis.

September 23, 2018

Autumn

I may pass tonight
into a land
of fruit trees
and fermenting apples.
It is autumn in the heavens.
The Natives harvest
and smoke their meats
draw cool waters
from fresh streams.

Fall

It is autumn:
Death shakes his rattle.
He sings his song
of slow passing.
It is his season
of prayer.

He kneels before me
a bitter-grape drink
on his breath,
soft bones loosely tied to his hair.

Death hums in the womb
of my ear.
He makes love to me.
All night, the rain.
In the morning, a damp horse.
We canter.

September 24, 2018
Gifts

For the first couple of years I lived in Cambridge, I worked at the Knotty Pine, which was a popular restaurant, bake shop and gift shop in Preston. It was an attractive stone building set on the Speed River. I was the head cashier in the gift shop and did a little of the buying. In many ways, it was an ideal job, as it was a pleasant environment, low pressure, and the hours were part-time. It allowed me to run my father's stone house for him and to write. The owners were good to me and offered me free meals during my shifts. I enjoyed their food. The only downside to the job was that I often worked until 11:00 at night, and I was bored at times. Business had slowed over the years, due to many factors, including competition. It was a long-standing family-owned business, but sometimes we would only sell a few items on a given day in the gift shop: a package of napkins, a chunk of fudge or a candle, for instance. I had the opportunity to become the manager, but I didn't think my health would allow me to work full-time, and I left shortly after. It was a good move, as the whole establishment closed a couple of months later.

The building was sold and transformed into a business called The Pines that focused on catered events like weddings. It was redecorated, and the exterior was painted. It looked lovely. I rented the facility for a book launch years later. My book was called *Oh My Goddess* (Serengeti Press, 2004) and my friend SMP— who ran the little publishing house, graciously organized it for me. We transformed the space into a spiritual setting to give thanks to the feminine God. I bought dozens of candles, and we placed them throughout the fountain I had stared at by the hour when I worked in the gift shop. We dimmed the lights and played opera music in the background. Guests enjoyed hors d'oeuvres and drinks. I wore a black dress and read at a podium from the small book. The event was a success and taught me that one's fate can take ironic twists.

September 25, 2018
Chiron

Chiron is a minor planet that was not discovered until 1977. Astrologically, it is considered a comet, a messenger who can bring physical healing, spiritual transformation and rejuvenation. But it has a maverick orbit and takes 50 years to circle the sun. If one has not processed earlier concerns associated with mid-life crisis, it can upset the status quo, wreak havoc and even bring health issues.

According to Greek mythology, Chiron was a gentle and wise Centaur, a healer, astrologer, philosopher and teacher who ironically could not heal his own wounds. And so, in our natal chart Chiron is symbolized as "the wounded healer." Chiron's placement in our horoscope can point to a core wound or hurt that may take most of our lives to work through. Our challenge is to assimilate what we have encountered. By knowing where Chiron lies in our chart, we can begin healing — physically, emotionally, mentally and spiritually — more consciously and with intention. This placement can also reveal our greatest spiritual strengths and healing powers. Chiron is both the wound and the salve. As we face our own issues, we gain wisdom we can pass on to others, for Chiron represents the area in our lives that can teach us the most.

There are sites on the Internet that can help you to identify where Chiron falls in your personal horoscope. Each of the twelve houses of a chart rules certain areas of life including relationships, ideas and circumstances. I have Chiron in the Twelfth House, for instance, which rules soul growth and secrets. As a result, I have difficulty processing sensitivities, had a parent who suffered from mental illness but am strong in spiritual leadership.

September 28, 2918
Little Dreads

I am alone in the waiting room of the Mental Health Clinic at my local hospital. I notice the sound of a heating ventilator. Now a huge fellow — tall and wide and tattooed — makes an appointment for November 14th at 1:00. He types it into his phone. Another guy says he has come for his inoculation. He is two days late. He has been ill. A young Black woman and a White woman sit close to me. The Black woman is fussing with her hair. She says her braids are too tight. The White woman seems interested. She talks to her about hair chemicals.

I wonder what these people discuss behind closed doors, what meds they might take. I have brought a list of matters to present to Dr. A—, mostly about writing and how to find a mate. When my mother passes, I will be alone. I am shy and slow of speech when I speak to her, but I am not a medical priority: as I leave, she says she will see me in three months. I want to tell her I have Chiron in the Twelfth House, but the session is over then. Outside, the Black woman is smiling but seems to be tearing her hair out. I wonder if she is sensitive to spirits too. The little dreadlocks like antennae on her head.

October 1, 2018
Doors

Once I was terribly short on cash and most gratefully received a phone call from a fellow who owned a small publishing company and was looking for an editor for his newsletters. For a few weeks, I reported faithfully to his office in Hespeler, in the north end of Cambridge. He was recently separated from his wife who remained in their big home with their four children. G— had a smart condo he had decorated with modern leather furniture and contemporary art. He drove a Ferrari with a licence plate that read "2Sexy." G—'s wife D— still worked for him and was pivotal in running their successful business. She seemed devoted to their family. Their children were in high school, and it was located across the street from their office. They often dropped in during lunch hour or after school to visit with their parents. G— ran a fairly-relaxed environment. There was a kitchen with coffee and snacks and a stereo that played rock music. His favourites were Rod Stewart and the Rolling Stones. G— was a short, stocky man with long well-groomed hair he coloured auburn. He often wore new running shoes. D— was a tall, slim woman who styled her dark hair in a short do and always looked clean and pretty. G— kept a black and white portrait of her on his desk despite their marital troubles.

Part of my duty as editor was to report to G— regularly in his closed office. He was a reflective fellow who appreciated art, wrote poetry and was interested in religion and spirituality. He once told me that he thought doorways were significant locations and that he had, in fact, met D—for the first time in a portal many years before on a rainy day. Despite his spiritual connection to her, G— began asking me to his condo regularly and inviting himself to my house in the country. I only agreed to drive to his home once, to deliver some important papers. He gave me a tour and stressed a few times that he had his own Jacuzzi. I became increasingly uncomfortable working at this company. I would meet with G— in his office and receive special attention and then walk out of his door into an open area where his significant other D— was seated at a desk. They were both Scorpios, a sign I consider to be strong and almost deadly when they are provoked to use their scorpion stingers. I was a little afraid. I also objected to the hours. When the newsletter was about to go to print, he would work his staff, all of whom were women, past midnight and then phone us at home at 3:00 a.m. to review edits.

Around this time, I decided to return to the University of Toronto to study theology. Unfortunately, my courses there — which included Medieval Church History, Women and the Bible and Anglican Spirituality — did not help me to understand G—, or some of the other difficult individuals I have encountered. I relied on my father while he was alive. He had an ability to read people, especially their dark sides. I imagine he could see clouds heavy with sin above G— raining on my parade.

October 2, 2018
Darkness, Light

When my father developed Alzheimer's, I took him to the hospital in Kitchener, and he never came home. I lived in my apartment in his stone house in the country alone for a few months before I found tenants to rent the rest of the old mansion. The house and property were situated on the corner of Hwy #24, a busy route between Cambridge and Brantford, and a concession road. But I felt isolated. My dog, Bear, was really my only companion.

Around this time, Bear began waking up in the night and staring into the open door between my bedroom and the kitchen. He did this repeatedly. Shortly after this behaviour began, the television set woke me from sleep a few times. It came on by itself. Then I began to detect the odour of marijuana and Scotch in the bathroom. I don't smoke drugs or drink and was alone in the house, so this was another mystery. The heady scent rose from a corner of the room, and soon bugs appeared in that same area. Next, I was awakened in the night by a violent shaking of my mattress. It literally heaved into the air, and I was tossed to the ceiling. This occurred on several occasions.

While always interested in the paranormal, I sensed a darkness, and I was truly terrified. I didn't have access to the Internet yet and really didn't know who to contact for counsel and help. I began, though, by writing to my astrologer who was trained in India. He suggested chanting the word "Om," thought to be a word to describe a trio of Hindu gods, and the waking, dreaming and dreamless states of consciousness. Some say it is the most perfect sound in the Universe. But the ghosts didn't flee.

Then, I remembered meeting a professor at Wilfrid Laurier University who taught ritual studies. I phoned him at his office at the university one warm summer evening, and to my surprise he was there. He suggested I take something that had special meaning to me, making it into a kind of amulet and wearing it around my neck. I chose a small music box my father had given me. It played a little tune. I hung it over my nightgown. It didn't blow the ghouls from my space.

I decided to move into a hotel for a short time. I was packing a bag when there was a knock at the door. It was a friend of my father's, who I had only met once. E— was a Turkish man. He owned a coffee shop in Kitchener called Mr. Mugs. He couldn't understand my distress but said he would sleep on the couch for a night in my father's living room. He assured me he didn't have an ulterior motive. I agreed to his platonic proposition. I slept more peacefully that night. In the morning, E— pushed me on my old wooden swing attached to a huge maple tree. I relaxed a little as I pumped up and down in the morning air. Then we went for a walk up the concession road. At this point, E— reached for my clammy hand and began to express romantic intensions. He was much older than me, recently divorced and had a face like a waxed mannequin in Madame Tussaud's museum. I simply wasn't interested.

My anxiety returned. Next, I drove to Toronto in my old Mercury Tracer for an appointment with my former Jungian analyst L—. She was a medical doctor who practiced a mystical form of dream analysis. We sat in her office on the floor in a renovated building at College and Spadina. She burned a candle and incense and offered me a glass of cold water. "Bless me, April," she said. "I am afraid I cannot offer any help." I was despondent. I made the long journey home.

But when I arrived at the beleaguered house on the hill and opened the door to my country flat, ready to face the haunts, I was overwhelmed by the presence of holy light. It was like standing in a cathedral on Easter morning. The light was warm and streamed throughout the long space I called the green room. It radiated from my old potbellied stove and my pagan artifacts. It lit up my closet, beamed from the crosses and little bronze music box I used to trouble the darkness.

October 3, 2018
Gray's Balm

My father had long episodes of mania during which he often made odd purchases. When I was a girl, he bought the rights to a salve called Gray's Balm which was popular among a small clientele in Kitchener. He swore by its medicinal properties, though joked he had to remove cancer from the list of illnesses it could cure. He stored the boilers and huge vessels of syrup in a cabin by the pond on our property in the country. It all smelled like the waxy gunk he manufactured only once and sold in little white jars. When he developed Alzheimer's and was confined to a nursing home, I quietly cleaned the cabin and set the ingredients for Gray's Balm at the bottom of the driveway with other trash. But the odour of the ointment haunts me, and today I wrote a few lines of poetry:

My father's balm:
liniment for nasal catarrh
arthritic ache...
A jar of thick yellow stink.

Daddy's spirit
and his odd demands.
"Anoint yourself," he says.
"Your temples, your wrists
and the stem of your head."

Outside
the limbs of trees
their stiff joints
and their dry red leaves.

October 5, 2018
Flotsam

My parents divorced when I was 28. I was relieved at first. My mother moved to a smaller condo within the same building in Mississauga where we had all lived for many years. It was a special complex, set on an acre of groomed land. It offered panoramic views of Lake Ontario and two golf courses. We all enjoyed the flowers, swimming pool, tennis courts, art gallery and fishpond; and my mother delighted in the many parties and events the social committee there organized for the residents. My father returned to Kitchener, where he had been born and raised, and moved into his childhood home where his elderly mother still lived. He resumed a kind of adolescent life eating greasy eggs and sausage at Jimmy's Lunch, pork burgers at the Harmony on King St. and drinking copious cups of coffee. I called him the "donut-shop psychologist," as he made friends easily and dispensed advice over steaming mugs and crullers.

But when my grandmother died of cancer, he and his brother sold the family home, and around this time my father was admitted to the hospital. I lived in Toronto and was not well myself. We both lingered in our respective beds. I gave thanks to God for each small movement but lay there almost paralyzed with depression, and Dad received electroshock therapy. He never recovered fully, however. He couldn't wade through the wreckage of his life, or the tides of his mental illness. My lethargy lasted a few years and then returned in waves daily, murky waters I slowly learned to navigate.

October 6, 2018
Attacks

Around the time of my major illness, I developed panic attacks that rendered me almost speechless. I experienced energy that charged my neck and throat, travelled like an electric current into my skull. These power surges occurred frequently throughout my day. They made communicating about anything a challenge. At the University of Windsor, I attempted to socialize a little, but some of the students gossiped that I "was strange and hard to talk to." These whispers haunted me. My mind became a ghostly room, an attic with a dark presence.

October 6, 2018
Thanksgiving

It is a mild but rainy autumn day. Tomorrow is Thanksgiving Sunday. When I was a student at York University in my early 20's, I usually had a bad cold around this time. But my former boyfriend D—'s birthday is on October 12th, so we often made the long trip from Toronto to Ottawa to visit his family and to celebrate both occasions. Once we needed a cheap lift and lay in the back of a van for five hours. I met D—'s grandmother that day. She was an old Dutch woman, who suffered from dementia. She spoke to me in her mother tongue then poked me in the nose. D—'s mother hailed from Glasgow, Scotland. She called me a "Georgy Girl," a term I never understood, even when I Googled it years later. She was a kind nursing student at the time, who offered me a piece of her prized pottery collection.

D— and I usually went dancing at a club in Hull on a Saturday night and the next morning had breakfast at Bagel Bagel in the ByWard Market. Sometimes, we would have a special coffee at Café Bohemian. But I was uncomfortable when the manager, a French fellow, flirted with D—.

D— is a successful industrial designer now who lives in Montreal with his lovely French wife and their beautiful daughter. They purchased and renovated an old Laudromat, and it was so hip when they completed it that the *Montreal Gazette* wrote an article on them and included a spread of photos of their unique home. It seems to me they have a lot to be thankful for on this holiday of gratitude.

I give thanks for the basics: shelter, groceries, medicine, a car...I wanted desperately to be a writer when I was a student at York University, and most days I pound away at my laptop making use of favourite words. Today, it is "gourds."

Earlier I went grocery shopping and made note of a Rastafarian fellow I had once seen in the cheese department. I also noted the fresh-produce section, with its newly harvested squash, gourds and carrots. I am an Earth sign and appreciate her dark womb, the bounty she heaves from her loins. I will never bear a child like D—s wife, but today I cradle a pumpkin like a newborn.

October 8, 2018
Reverend Blue Jeans

Recently I Googled an old friend and discovered his obituary. He died a year ago at the age of 60. I met M— in Divinity school at the University of Toronto. He was a very-intelligent rock-and-roll dude who was hell-bent on becoming an Anglican priest. He had been a singer, song writer and musician in a successful Canadian band. He still wore his hair in a mullet and usually sported jeans and cowboy boots. M— brought his guitar on retreats and sang classic rock songs to the faculty and other students. We sometimes chatted outside the big wooden door that led to an ancient hallway and the chapel where we worshipped early each morning. He was a heavy smoker, and I remember the puffs he blew into the chilly air. We often disagreed about theological and other issues. I was an ardent feminist and he frequented a bar and grill in North Toronto where he often flirted with the waitresses and eyed their "tight sweaters." He was married with two children, but once said he thought we would be great together. I flew from his car like a bat out of hell.

He was ordained and rose through the ranks of the Church. He seemed to have had a crisis of faith, however. His obituary did not mention his clerical career. Instead, it read that he was devoted to social justice issues and his new wife and dog. I think his true calling was to write and record mystical rock songs for his risen Lord. I imagine Jesus strumming along on his air guitar.

October 8, 2018
La Balance

Last night, my mother watched a movie starring Doris Day. She worked in a circus. Mom liked the big elephant and white horses Doris balanced upon. Today is not colourful or carny. It is raining outside, and there is a thick fog. It is holiday Monday, a slow chilly unfolding of autumn. We will have Rock Cornish hen for dinner and pumpkin tarts.

I read my horoscope early this morning when the light was dim. It is a month of excessive spending and emotion. I will feel rejected but shouldn't respond.

The sun is slowly breaking through the fog. It is in Libra, *La Balance*. I think of you C—, wonder where you are today. You are Taurus like me. I imagine you sleep late and dream of vegetables lying in a field damp with rain, farmers hauling baskets onto trucks. How heavy the harvest. I send you bright images to lift your spirits: clowns, their stupid pratfalls and shoes. Perhaps you will laugh in your sleep, giggle under the big top like Doris and my mom.

I offer Thanksgiving love to you, though my heart is a weird gourd.

October 9, 2018
Editors

I was a researcher and fact-checker at *Maclean's* magazine in Toronto for two years in the 1990s. It was a full-time job but condensed into four days. We worked about 12 hours on Fridays when the weekly magazine went to bed. I wasn't always well enough to sustain my energy for that length of time. I also wasn't understood by some of the more aggressive editors there. One was short tempered and angry and made derogatory comments about poets as we sat together correcting stories at a computer. It was a stressful job, especially when there was a war or tragedy that required verifying information overseas.

My days improved, however, when I was given my own section to cover. I became the entertainment researcher and enjoyed checking film reviews and stories on authors and artists. The entertainment editor was kind, and she sometimes took me to operas and other events with free passes we received. But when news came that there were budget shortages and impending cutbacks, I was the first to lose my job, as I was the most recent employee to be hired. The managing editor broke the news to me in his dimly lit office. He rarely acknowledged me and was brief with his stern message. I don't think he delivered the layoff with a sympathetic heart for the lights flickered as he spoke, and for a short time we sat in the dark.

October 9, 2018
Medical Arts

I am at Dr. Beth's again with my mother. The same pair is here — the worker and the young girl who studies social skills. I have brought a snack this time, a bag of dried apricots.

A nice-looking doctor calls a woman into his office. A stethoscope hangs around his neck like a black snake. It reminds me of the symbol for medicine: a serpent-entwined staff reminiscent of a rod wielded by the Greek god Asclepius who was associated with healing and medical arts. He was a son of Apollo. Wikipedia tells me that in honour of Asclepius, non-venomous snakes were often used in healing rituals. They crawled around freely on the floor of dormitories where the ill and injured slept. Later in temples, dreams or visions were interpreted by a priest who prescribed the appropriate therapy. Others used sacred dogs to lick the wounds of the sick.

Here comes my mom. She is waving a prescription.

October 10, 2018
Workshops

When I was still a student at York University in Toronto, I landed a job at TVOntario. I was working toward an Honours B.A. at the time in mass communications and English, and my employers seemed impressed by this double major. I was assigned to the Educational Services department. Most of my colleagues there had been schoolteachers and joined TVO to provide workshops for other teachers in how to use programming in the classroom. They travelled all over the province with videotapes and accompanying print material. They also trained teachers on how to give these workshops, and they freelanced for TVO. My job was to complete appropriate paperwork associated with these events and ensure that the workshop specialists received their materials.

I also wrote a newsletter that was mailed to them. I worked at TVOntario for three years, but I was haunted by the idea of being a poet. My best friend there supported the idea. She said to "follow your bliss." She was a Jewish woman from Montreal who painted, practiced yoga and ate a macrobiotic diet.

When I resigned from TVO to attend Concordia University's graduate program in creative writing, my father had a bird. He wanted me to have a stable life and steady income.

But I don't regret my decision. I had a cute apartment in Montreal, flourished in the city's culture and wrote like a fiend. My creative thesis was picked up by Cormorant Books shortly after I graduated, and the short stories I wrote in a prose workshop were eventually published in a collection by Black Moss Press.

I have since joined a group called the TVO Primetimers, mostly for retired employees. They usually meet twice a year. For a time, I had a good visit at these events with my friend Jack Livesley who sadly passed away last year at the age of 90. He was an English teacher who became a television producer and on-air host of educational programs. After retiring, he wrote books of funny poetry.

The editor of the TVO Primetimers newsletter has graciously published a few of my poems and even illustrated them with inspiring photographs. In this way, I received some of the best of both worlds.

October 11, 2018
The Rock

Today, I learned my former handyman at our country house passed away almost 15 years ago. B— was a retired fellow from Bell Island, Newfoundland whose big, meaty hands were put to good use at our decaying property, though I had trouble paying him from my wages at the gift shop. But he arrived almost daily in coveralls and an insulated hat looking for little jobs. I gradually projected father feelings onto this capable man.

My father could barely light a match with his soft, clammy hands.

But B—, though a devout Catholic, liked his screech and began arriving three sheets to the wind wielding an electric chainsaw to chop wood for my potbellied stove. We argued on the telephone and he called me "aggressive." I thought he would contact me and apologize, but he never did. I mourned when it was clear I wouldn't hear his Newfie expressions again. I remember plodding through deep snow and leaning against an old tree for awhile. "I'll drop over 'round by and by," I heard him say in my mind as I had a good cry. Only imagined the Celtic lilt of "Stay where you're to 'till I comes where you're at" on the winter wind.

October 11, 2018
Ocular Eye Clinic

A woman with a huge bag of coloured wool hooks blue strands around a wide, plastic ring in the waiting room. "You can make a hat in no time," she tells me. "It will be a toque." An old man fingers his cellphone. He wears a cap that reads, "I'm Following Jesus."

I read the clinic motto behind the front desk: "Our Vision is <u>Your</u> Vision," it says.

October 12, 2018
Script

My father's cousin J— was a friendly eccentric, a chain-smoking Aries. I enjoyed her Mars energy. She worked for years as an insurance adjuster, helping people who had suffered catastrophes. But I was most interested in her hobby — handwriting analysis. When I went to visit her on Weber St. in Kitchener, I usually tucked a letter or postcard from a friend or relative in my purse and asked her to share her insights into their characters. She told me one fellow I knew, a professor, had tremendous powers of concentration, an eco-feminist was concerned with recycling, my father was as stubborn as a pig on ice, my mother generous, and I was intuitive. She took courses but seemed to have an innate sensitivity to the implications of penmanship. She passed away in the house where she lived for over 50 years a decade or so ago, but I still think of her sometimes when I am dashing off a note or writing a poem — crossing my T's and looping my O's.

October 14, 2018
Basic Needs

I dreamed this morning of a fellow I met a year ago. S— was a regular at the singles dances. He looked me up on Facebook and asked me out for coffee. In the dream, he lives in one room with his brother who roots through my purse and steals my car. Perhaps this brother figure is his shadow, for I sensed S— was a gold digger. He seemed strapped for cash: he worked as an extra in film and television and delivered pizzas to cover the rent. He still lived with his ex-girlfriend, though he assured me it was over romantically. We met at Monigram Coffee Roasters in Galt, a nice café, then walked by the Grand River. He was bossy and self-absorbed. I didn't see him again, though he wanted to take me to the waterfalls in Hamilton if I wore a dress on the date. In the dream, I am searching for my Chevy, my handbag and my keys. I have lost the basics: what I truly need.

October 15, 2018
The Balm

Yesterday, I attended an autumn celebration given by The Ontario Poetry

Society (TOPS) in Oakville. The café, which was situated by a yacht club, offered an expansive view of Lake Ontario. It was called Taste of Columbia and served delicious Spanish food and coffee. I met a poet from India who is also an alternative nutrition expert. She taught me that our sleep patterns can affect our weight. She was very personable. Others were also supportive and kind.

I launched my new book, *Out of Darkness, Light,* which is about a congregation of fictional women who worship by the Grand River here in Cambridge. I have a sense that I confront listeners' religious convictions, and they sometimes resist. Having studied women and religion at university, however, I believe it is time to thoroughly acknowledge the feminine in our spiritual practices and to also salve the Earth and her scars. My book is meant for women and men who wish to anoint themselves with the healing spirit of the Great Mother, the Goddess of balm.

October 16, 2018
Ghosts

I began writing poetry when I was a teenager. I had a boring job as a receptionist in a condominium on weekends when I was in high school. Very few people visited the lobby where I worked, and the telephone rarely rang. And so, I began to scribble lines of verse on company letterhead. My first piece was about pretense. I was quite unhappy in those days and wore a kind of false smile to my school where some of the kids had embraced Christ and were born again. Two boys were the sons of evangelist David Mainse, the founder of *100 Huntley St.*, a fundamentalist Christian television program in Toronto. I was still young and had not found a spiritual path, but I found this conservative and evangelical. Today, I read the ministry was investigated for inappropriate use of donated funds.

My first poem was a real dog, but it was a form I found compelling. I continued to pen little lines. My best friend at school was Eliza Clark, a gifted Gemini who desperately wanted to be a novelist. She encouraged me for many years, especially at York University where we both took creative writing workshops with well-known authors. She continued to write after graduation, publishing quirky novels with well-established publishers and receiving nominations for prestigious awards such as the Stephen Leacock Medal for Humour and the coveted Giller Prize. Poets generally do not receive as much attention, but I have won many contests and been shortlisted for a couple of awards.

I am a shy and quiet person and find that writing is my favourite form of communication. Poetry allows me to explore meanings in the unfolding of everyday life in a way that conversation does not. Today for instance, I take note of the design on my window: patterns like apparitions pressed to the glass. The way they cry against my pane. The warm ghosts of autumn: spirits, their haunted mouths like cups of steam.

October 17. 2018
The Blue Angel

Each Monday, after prose workshop at Concordia University in Montreal, my professor and fellow students bundled into winter coats and made a short trek to a local tavern called the Blue Angel on Drummond St. The course was held in the evenings and so we would arrive around 9:30 p.m. The Blue Angel was a country-western bar that served huge jugs of beer. We quaffed copious jars and waxed poetic on the writer's life and craft. At midnight, we stuffed ourselves with free hot dogs.

The next morning, I would worry about what I said the night before under the influence. I didn't know then that I suffered mental-health issues and that the beer had both powerful stimulating and depressive effects on my brain chemistry.

Almost 30 years ago, I stopped drinking entirely. Since then, I've wondered many times about the role of alcohol at universities and colleges. I think that excessive drinking is not only a rite of passage during frosh week that leads to serious behavioural and health risks, but it can have detrimental effects on students throughout their academic careers — even dire consequences. For instance, in 2010 two alcohol-related deaths were reported at Queen's University and led to a coroner's investigation. The next year, a student at Acadia University died of alcohol poisoning during orientation week.

Since then, some post-secondary schools have conducted reports on harmful drinking and implemented awareness campaigns. The challenge, however, is to extend policies and controls to university and college communities and cities with high drinking rates.

I recall a recording of Patsy Cline crooning "I Fall to Pieces" at the Blue Angel. Though a love song, I still equate the title with those nights I was in my cups.

October 18, 2018
Evening News

I still dream of M—, a journalist at *Maclean's*, though it has been almost 30 years since I worked there. I once showed my Jungian analyst a photo of M— taken in the Middle East, and she labelled her "an animus woman," driven by unconscious masculine energy. Some at the magazine defined her as having a perfect balance of the feminine and masculine. Perhaps this is the reason my unconscious mind presents her to me so often at night. I still struggle to develop those qualities we traditionally identify as manly. M— enjoyed cigarettes and a good stiff drink after work, but it was her ability to travel to dangerous locations and report world news that I would like to bring to light in me.

M— was kind and drove me to a party once, and later took me to dinner when I was the victim of budget cuts. She was married and eventually had a little boy, a child she adored so much she resigned her position as a bureau chief.

I'm not sure how to develop my inner M— and heal the masculine images in my psychology. They present themselves in my dreams as disabled — confined to wheelchairs, hobbling on canes and prosthetic legs. Perhaps I will take a walk now and meditate on a steady gait.

October 21, 2018
Mother's

On a manic high my father once had a vision of establishing a tearoom. He went to Quebec and had a dozen12-foot-long pine-tables shipped to our garage, as well as boxes of hurricane lamps and other antiques he fancied. When he came down from his mania, he seemed to have little interest in his dream, and my mother was burdened with the task of clearing the furnishings from our suburban house. Her sister suggested contacting Mother's Pizza, a chain known for decorating their restaurants in 19th-century style. My mother thought this was a marvellous idea and did a little research. The owner came quite a distance to our Mississauga home and brought a truck and a cheque. He cleared Dad's "warehouse" and his vision from our family's troubled unconscious.

October 22, 2018
"Bob" Quixote

Yesterday, my mother and I attended a performance of *Man of La Mancha* at the Hamilton Family Theatre in Cambridge. While not a typically feel-good musical, it really spoke to me. It is based on Cervantes' 17th century novel, *Don Quixote,* an epic story and one of the first pieces of historical literature to be adapted to musical theatre. *Man of la Mancha* is designed as a play-within-a-play, set in the period of the Spanish Inquisition when poet/historical author Miguel de Cervantes and his manservant are imprisoned and awaiting trial. His fellow inmates seize his belongings, including a manuscript he has written. He suggests holding a mock trial, to determine whether it should be returned to him. He proves the merit of his written work through a re-enactment in the form of a play, enlisting his fellow prisoners as actors. Cervantes takes the lead role of Alonso Quijano, an elderly nobleman who has lost his mind and believes he is a knight errant who should travel forth under the name of Don Quixote de La Mancha. He and his trusty squire, Sancho Panza, take to the road in a quest for adventure. They seek chivalry, goodness and innocence but encounter a world of violence and despair. Though madly mistaking a windmill for a giant and a rough inn for a castle, Don Quixote's visions transform his fellow prisoners. Moreover, an abused prostitute, the object of his affections, becomes a noblewoman. In doing so, he teaches us that a confused old man's delusions can lead to knighthood.

The production starred, Alex Mustakas as Quixote. Mustakas is a well-known actor, who also founded many "Drayton Theatres" throughout Southwestern Ontario and serves as their Artistic Director. His performance was stellar, and his singing voice soared in renditions of the stirring "Dulcinea" and the celebrated "Impossible Dream."

The play helped me heal a few memories of my father, Bob, I found embarrassing. For a few moments throughout the production, I imagined him as the odd, yet funny Don Quixote, Knight of the Woeful Countenance and me, his trusty squire. Battling forth in his white Buick, we transformed forlorn patrons of coffee shops and furniture stores, escorting them from darkness to light.

October 23, 2018
Deep Blue

My friend L— is on a Mediterranean cruise with her husband and soon will dock in Greece. I imagine them peering over the railing of the ship into the deep blue eye of the sea, a cyclops.

Three quarters of the Earth's body is covered by water.

I once took a trip in a submarine and watched the drama beneath the ocean: a theatre of creatures and fish.

"Water is history," the Canadian poet Gwendolyn MacEwen wrote. I wonder what L— reads in the ocean's great iris, as she gazes into it from the big boat.

October 24, 2018
Oshun

Years ago, when I lived in Toronto, my cousin A— and I attended a feminist spirituality workshop. We were asked to choose a tarot card from a Goddess deck, then dance in the spirit of that feminine deity. My card depicted the West African goddess Oshun, and I have had an interest in her ever since. I even acquired a framed poster of her image.

Oshun (also spelled Osun) is an orisha, a spirit, a deity or a goddess in a pantheon of over 400 gods in the Yoruba religion. The Yoruba people inhabit parts of modern-day Nigeria and Benin. Oshun is one of the most popular orishas and believed to be one of the first to be sent to Earth — the only female at that time, the matriarch. Oshun.is regarded principally as a goddess of love and sexual ecstasy. But she is also deity of sweet waters and is patron saint of the Oshun River in Nigeria. The Yoruba people dedicated a sacred grove that runs along the river to her. This dense forest contains 40 shrines, two palaces and many sculptures and works of art, and as a result was designated a UNESCO World Heritage site in 2005. Today, Oshun is still honoured in an annual two-week-long Nigerian festival. Every year, usually in August, Oshun devotees gather at the Oshun River to pay homage to her, make sacrifice, and ask for wealth, children and better health, for Oshun is regarded as a highly benevolent deity.

Oshun is said to be the protector and defender of the poor and the mother of all orphans. She is also regarded as a healer of the sick and the inspiration of song, music and dance. She is associated with sensuality and fertility and is central to women in West African culture. Those who desire children or who suffer issues of infertility often call upon her, for she is associated with the feminine power of women. She is sought after in times of drought and severe poverty and is depicted as a teacher who taught the Yoruba agriculture and how to achieve prosperity. She is also known as Yalode, the mother of wealth, due to her business skills and acumen.

Oshun taught the Yoruba the art of mysticism and divination using shells, as well as religious rituals involving songs, chants, possessions, tarots, visions and meditations passed on to her by her sweet yet powerful father Obatala, who is worshipped as the creator of Earth and sculptor of humanity from mud and clay.

Central to African traditions, Oshun was brought to the Americas during the African diaspora and was adopted into African pantheons and belief systems in those countries. But Oshun was also syncretized with Our Lady of Charity, patron saint of Cuba, and Our Lady of Aparecida, the patron saint of Brazil. In Trinidad she is associated with St. Philomena and the Hindu deity Mother Ganges.

In art, she is depicted like many of her counterparts from other religions — the Greek Aphrodite, for instance — as a young woman: beautiful, charming and sensual. In addition to her natural beauty, Oshun is also adorned with gold and brass jewelry, beads, mirrors and decorative fans. For it is claimed that she is attracted to glitter and shine. During her life as a mortal, she served as princess consort to a king. But in some fables and stories, she is rendered as a mermaid with a fish tail, perhaps as a reference to her as the goddess of fresh waters. Other myths describe her as one of the wives of Shango, the god of thunder. In one Yoruba story, she has a tempestuous temper, destroying crops by withholding waters, causing widespread droughts. In another myth, angered she sends down rain, nearly flooding the world. Yet once appeased, Oshun calls back the waters and saves the Earth.

Food offerings to Oshun could include sweet things such as fresh water, honey, white wine, oranges, or pumpkins, as well as incense and essential oils. Other offerings to her could be in the form of song, chant and meditation.

Oshun is also known as Laketi, "She who responds," because believers say she promptly answers prayers. One of her principal manifestations is possession. In such states, devotees seem to experience clarity, confidence and joy, as well as the power to fight injustice and irreverent behaviour against the gods. It is believed that when Oshun possesses her followers she flirts, dances and then weeps with them — because the world falls short in its beauty and love. Her manifestations of love include being the source of sweet waters and motherhood. It is thought one can learn much about her many moods by studying the rivers, streams and brooks she rules.

October 27, 2018
Veils

Last night, a waning gibbous moon, the great bone of her skull wrapped in black fabric, her pale face bruised. I dreamed of my Muslim doctor and her *hijab*. I was in a pharmacy full of women draped in cloth and shawls. I wore one, too.

Tomorrow, I will travel to Toronto for the launch of my book *Out of Darkness, Light*. It will likely rain, they say. Somewhere the moon, the damp weave of her *dupatta*, will perform *Sajda*, perhaps. But I will read to her a poem of pagan prayer and ritual, the medicine of my ladies. Their hair loose and pretty in my book, though I will imagine them bandaged in hats.

October 30, 2018
Launch

En route to my book launch, my cab tried to turn right onto Augusta Avenue in Kensington Market in Toronto, but the road was closed for "Pedestrian Sunday." The driver got out of the car and tried to negotiate with a fellow at the barricade. I heard him say, "I have to get the old lady through." But the fellow wouldn't open the barrier. I walked in the rain from Dundas to College with luggage full of books. When I reached the restaurant, it wasn't open yet, so I stood in a doorway watching people smoke reefers of marijuana, as they strolled in the rain.

Poets Don Gutteridge and John Di Leonardo and I read in a dark room decorated for Halloween. We were recorded for a radio show at Queen's University in Kingston. Hidden Brook Press sold books for us at a long table in the back. After, we stayed for dinner. I sat with a Polish poet/artist who told me her sister was recently diagnosed with early-onset Alzheimer's. K—, blonde and lovely, seemed so sad. But then told me of her grandchildren. "They are beautiful," she said.

The waiter wore a little toque. His first name was Charles, like my father. My father faded like K's— sister. Wandering the narrow hall of the nursing home like a ghost. Haunting me before he passed. I wonder about my own memories. Will they rise like puffs from a toker's mouth?

October 31, 2018
Bonfires

Today is Halloween, a holiday that dates back 2,000 years to an ancient Celtic festival called Samhain (pronounced sow-in) which marked the end of summer and the harvest and the beginning of the dark, cold winter. The Celts associated it with death and thought that the veil between the world of the living and of the dead was thin on the night of October 31st and that ghosts returned to earth then. They lit huge sacred bonfires and wore costumes, typically of animal heads and skins, to ward off these ghosts, for they were thought to cause trouble and damage crops. But it was also believed that the presence of these spirits aided Celtic priests in predicting the winter weather ahead and in telling fortunes.

In the eighth century, Pope Gregory III declared that November 1st would be designated as a day to honour all saints and martyrs. Soon the Church incorporated some of the traditions of Samhain into All Souls' Day and celebrated with big bonfires, parades and costumes of saints, angels and devils. The evening before became known as All Hollows Eve, and later Halloween.

Our modern-day tradition of "trick or treating" probably dates back to early All Souls' Day parades in England when the poor would beg for food and families would offer them pastries called "soul cakes" in return for prayers for their dead.

Today, I think of my late father who lit bonfires in the backyard of our suburban house in Mississauga when I was a child. He raked leaves and other brush until great plumes of smoke rose like spells through the wooded streets.

November 2, 2018
Istanbul

This morning, I discovered some notes about E— who I interviewed 20 years ago. I was interested in his heritage. He was born in Istanbul — where the Black Sea, the Sea of Marmara and the Aegean meet. He often went fishing for small mackerels and sardines and other fish the seasons brought, sometimes in the Golden Horn. This is an inlet that geographically separates the ancient city from the rest of Istanbul, a sheltered harbour that protected Greek, Roman and other commercial ships for thousands of years.

Today, Istanbul is a busy city of 15.5 million people. It is very romantic, he told me, reaching for my hand.

"Constantine cried when he lost the city he loved," said E—. He was the first Roman emperor to convert to Christianity. "There are many legends," he said. For instance, there is scholarly debate about how "Christian" his rule and observances were. Some believe that he continued to worship mythological divinities and to practice pagan ceremonies.

But years later, I learned that Constantine once had a vision of a cross of light in the heavens, above the sun. Later, in a dream, Christ appeared to him with the same sign and commanded him to make a likeness of it and to use it as protection in all conflicts with his enemies. And so, he called together workers and described to them the cross he had seen, telling them to represent it in gold and precious stones. The emperor made use of this sign of salvation as a safeguard against hostile powers and commanded that other similar symbols should be carried at the head of all his armies.

The medieval church upheld Constantine the Great as a paragon of virtue, while secular rulers identified him as a prototype of imperial legitimacy and character. Later, beginning in the Renaissance, there were more critical reviews of him and his reign, due to the rediscovery of anti-Constantinian sources. Scholars in modern and recent eras have attempted to balance these extremes.

Today, E— enjoys fly fishing on the Grand River in Kitchener. "It is relaxing therapy," he told me. I imagine him casting his rod into the shallow green water, as though the Black Sea, the scent of Turkish coffee in his memory. The grounds were read by fortune tellers who divined the future in signs and symbols. A Muslim country today but haunted by Constantine and his prophetic vision.

November 4, 2018
The Colour Purple

When I was a child of three, I remember my father lying in an ambulance. He had been travelling icy roads in Northern Ontario with a friend, both peddling lines of furniture to a store in Blind River. An oil tanker jackknifed and slammed into their Chrysler on a narrow highway. My father was severely injured. The tender flesh of his face fell away from its bones, he broke his ankle and the rib that arched over the pond of his heart. I remember him later in his master bedroom. He often called to me for comfort and succour. His cheek was purple and packed with gauze. The cast on his leg a plaster burden I scribbled upon with crayons.

November 5, 2018
Hospital Policies

Today, I am sick as a dog. My fat head throbs as though a slow clock about to sound its morning alarm. Fever lies across my brow like a damp rag. I hallucinated all night in my little iron bed, dreamed of a hospital and a psychiatric patient. She reminded me of a friend who attempted suicide in the cold waters of the Grand. Later, nurses hid her shoes — swollen and caked with mud. I brought her miniature roses in a glass vase. The jar was confiscated by staff, and so she cradled the wet bouquet like a new babe, pink and blooming in her sad arms.

November 6, 2018
Riverbed

For 40 years, my womb — the mouth of a river that has since run dry. Scarred by the flow of blood on its bed of bone.

I recall tea and prayers to the goddess who squatted in me, the long drag of her red gown. I remember the little blemishes we anointed, the gauze of her sacrifice, the fatigue like a heavy stone.

November 8, 2018
Encryption

Yesterday, my email account was hacked and strange messages asking for a "favour" and soliciting money for a "niece" were sent to hundreds of my contacts with my name on them. I hardly slept. This morning I open myself to another day, a new password on my heart.

November 9, 2018
Cameo Appearance

Yesterday, I met a woman who is a gemologist and who works with antique jewelry. She is also psychic and able to feel the vibrations of people who once wore the old watches and rings she sells. This is called psychometry. She examined my friend's ring and determined it was of the Victorian era. "A lovely cameo," she said, "carved from shell." She Googled similar pieces and confirmed her appraisal. Then she held the gold ring in her sensitive hand and said it once belonged to a dark-haired woman who wore it rolled in the style of the era. "She was a strong lady," she said, "learned, perhaps a governess…She immigrated to Canada." I imagined this woman, the classic cameo adorning a long shapely finger. Perhaps a gift from her husband: a portrait of a pale lady engraved in an oval frame, raised in relief against a black stone.

Today, I wear a ring my mother gave me for my 50th birthday. It is silver and hammered into three wavy bands. It symbolizes my family, three of us bound together on my dominant hand.

November 11, 2018
Wash and Wear

Yesterday, I attended a local church bazaar where I bought three second-hand bracelets and a smart watch with a brown-leather strap. I do not have the gift to read the energy of those who once owned these pieces but nevertheless believe they hold the vibrations of those who perhaps wore them close.

The gemologist I met recently advised me to wash used articles in clear water and then set them in the moonlight. The moon's energizing rays will cleanse them in a day or so, she said.

Later, I did a little research on the subject and learned that smudging with white sage, rinsing with rose water and setting a used item on a bed of sea salt in sunlight for a few days will also remove energies from previous owners. This is important because jewelry, gems and crystals can attract positive and negative energies and hold them until cleansed.

I learned, too, that it is sometimes necessary to rinse away the emotional baggage some articles might carry — a ring from an ex, a bracelet from a friend who did you wrong, for instance. Cleansing these pieces and placing them before the sacred altar of the moon or the sun can help imbue them with new meaning. Wearing these items, perhaps crafted from metal and stone, can also aid in healing processes. They absorb pain and promote new attitudes if they are worn then cleansed regularly. I imagine the moon wiping them clean with her soft cloth and beams.

November 11, 2018

Poppies

My heart is a red flower
planted in the field
of my chest.
All night I did not sleep

for guns fired in my mind,
though this morning
larks fly
and quietly nest.

I was a poet
reading "In Flanders Fields"
in the dim,
imagining Lieutenant Colonel John McCrae
penning near a dressing station,
his face tired but calm.

I too said
a few passages from
"Order of the Burial of the Dead"
for I have read of soldiers
who lay down in Afghanistan:
Canadian women and men.

But all night I paced
a field of poppies.
They blossomed
then died.
And bloomed again.

November 13, 2018
Year of the Horse

At the church bazaar, Ernie served lemon meringue pie with a quivering hand. Donny poured coffee. He is from Newfoundland. My mother worked at the knitting table, selling afghans and wool gloves for children. I was tempted to buy her a small Chinese horse made of iron. I believe

Mom is an old soul, often an Oriental woman.

The horse was set among cheap vases and knick-knacks in a room beyond the parish hall. I imagined it was formed in an early dynasty by a child who turned it over fire. She wore a simple dress, perhaps fashioned from silk. I admired its mandarin collar in my mind. But at $6 the horse seemed overpriced among the other items marked at $1 or so. I only imagined my mother opening it on her birthday, her discerning hands determining its true value.

November 15, 2018
The A-Team

Yesterday, I attended a lecture at my women's Probus club given by Rick Green of the CBC comedy hit *The Red Green Show*. Rick suffers from Attention Deficit Hyperactivity Disorder (ADHD). He gave a lucid and compelling talk about this largely misunderstood neurological condition and his experiences and struggles living with it.

Considered to be either a brain or mental health disorder, ADHD interferes with daily functioning. It is characterized by distinct sets of symptoms that all work together to form a single condition. Inattention, hyperactivity and impulsivity are the three areas in which a person with ADHD often has trouble. Rick described himself as having a Ferrari brain and Model T brakes. He listed some common issues associated with ADHD including making careless errors, losing things, trouble listening, impatience, fidgeting with hands or feet, blurting out answers, having too much on the go, pacing while thinking, procrastination, poor memory, extreme moods and emotions.

Researchers have found that these children and adults are short of certain neurotransmitters, but the diagnosis is often messy, and doctors sometimes assume it is depression. The good news is that there are medications available now, and several genes have been isolated as the root cause. Lower levels of dopamine are also believed to be behind the symptoms of ADHD.

Rick explained that those with this condition tend to be driven as though by a motor. Some flourish in high-stress jobs. For example, he said that many members of the military have this syndrome and even several astronauts. Rick is creative and innovative and has had success in comedy, television, science programming, public speaking and writing. He has won awards such as the Order of Ontario and the Order of Canada.

Diagnosed at age 47, he attributes medication, mindfulness practice, meditation, exercise and a diet high in carbohydrates as helpful in controlling his condition. He cited the case of a fellow who worked as a janitor and after diagnosis and treatment became a lawyer. These are success stories, indeed, as the average ADHD sufferer receives about 20,000 more negative messages than an average person: accusations like 'What the heck were you thinking?' Car accidents, divorce, bankruptcy, sexually transmitted diseases and a shorter lifespan are also sometimes issues for these people; as are gambling, shopping, caffeine, sex and alcohol addictions. Many also find it difficult to finish high school and about 40% of them have learning disorders like dyslexia. But Rick and his son (who also has ADHD) both have university degrees, and his son works in the field of robotics. Still, having ADHD "is like a wrestling match with an invisible opponent," laughed Rick Green, the comic.

November 17, 2018
Sacraments

Yesterday was my mother's 89th birthday. My Aunt B— and Cousin J— joined us for a celebration at the Country Club. My mother brought along a photograph of herself as a baby. Her fine shaggy hair framed her round face, and her loose gown hung over her plump new body. I, too, was a baby once, born Caesarean section at Toronto General Hospital, drawn from my mother's wound by an obstetrician named Dr. Bean. I was in an incubator for days as a result. My father was at a wedding toasting the bride and groom. My mother dozed in a roomful of pink roses. And so, I imagine myself in the warmth of the glass box like a loaf of bread in an oven. A small birthmark like a stain of Communion wine under my right thumb. Only a nurse lifting me to the light of the room.

November 18, 2018
Raphael

I am reading old journal entries from 1989, when I lived in Montreal. Raphael, a Black fellow who owned the Laundromat where I washed my clothes, told me he was the only man to be born without lenses on his eyes. They looked like peeled grapes. He said he danced at the Forum with Ziggy Marley, had been dancing since he was nine. His woman took $34,000 from him. I wondered if he was legally blind. Later, I read a quote from Belgian artist René Magritte (1898-1967): "'If the dream is a translation of waking life, waking life is also a translation of the dream.'"

November 20, 2018
Ötzi

The oldest discovery of tattooed human skin was found on the body of Ötzi the Iceman, a prehistoric mountaineer who likely lived in the Bronze Age around 3,300 B.C. Ötzi was discovered at a height of more than 10,000 feet in the Austrian Alps in 1991 by a pair of German tourists who were hiking in the mountains. The frozen body was remarkably well preserved by glacial conditions. His tissue, bones and organs yielded details from his life — his age, height and weight, for instance. And in 2001, scientists announced that the Iceman probably died from wounds inflicted by an arrowhead found in his left shoulder. He was still clad in his original primitive clothing, including an animal-hide coat and grass cape. But it is the tattoos decorating Ötzi that truly fascinate me.

Scientists who have studied the Iceman have hypothesized that the dozens of lines and crosses offered therapeutic benefits rather than simply serving as decorative body art. The tattoos, which were created through small incisions and traced with charcoal, align with the ankles, wrists, knees and lower back, locations commonly associated with acupuncture treatments. As a result, researchers speculated that Ötzi's community knew of the practice 2,000 years or so before it was believed to have first emerged in Asia.

Various herbs and medicines were also found by his remains which have led scientists to believe that Ötzi was a member of a society who practiced relatively advanced healthcare treatments. Plants found amongst the Iceman's belongings suggest a portrait of a surprisingly sophisticated society. A fern found in his stomach could have served as a tapeworm remedy, and traces of moss may be remnants of bandages. Birch fungus tied to the leather bands of Ötzi's tools may have treated inflammation or acted as an antibiotic. Other tools Ötzi bore suggested that these early peoples might have practiced surgery.

I think God preserved this primitive man to teach us about the roots of some of our modern-day practices. I imagine an early physician treating Ötzi's body roughly 5,300 years ago, a pharmacy of plants in the doctor's rough sack. Perhaps Ötzi was stretched upon a plateau while the surgeon carved a simple cross into the thin skin of his chest.

November 21, 2018

Tree Trimming

We have had early snowfall this November, today it is very windy and cold. Residents in my apartment building are decorating a Christmas tree and hanging ornaments from the chandelier in the lobby. I am weak today and wonder whether I will be strong enough to do something similar in my little living room. I didn't sleep well and dreamed of an early life with C—. We were Native Canadians shivering in our skins. The moon above: a god we worshipped with our blue lips. We were pagans who hung our prayers on trees.

November 22, 2018

X

I read an old journal from my life in Montreal. It is dated January 28, 1990. "V— is pregnant...She is so calm and mellow but says she will have an abortion. Later, on February 9, 1990: "V— had her abortion yesterday. She sounded fine on the phone. But I want to use the image of her standing in Café X, a spot of red paint on the tile upon which she stood."

November 23, 2018
Sisters

I found some notes today from 1992 when I was writing my book *The Weight of Wings*. I have a character named Esther's Sister. This fictional woman watches Esther, who was confined to a wheelchair, pass away.

"When Esther dies, the nuns open the earth and lay her down in the dark hollow. Back into the womb, and the nuns there like midwives, asking God to pull her from the earth's belly and give her some milk. To pull her through the small place and to hold her: thin, broken Esther. The earth takes her shape: the weight of her body and bones.

They pile dirt over my sister and the prairie is swelled big, though Esther does not kick or turn. The nuns make the cross, then fly like crows."

November 24, 2018
Mother Superior

When I was in my late 20s, I travelled from Toronto to a Quebec retreat centre: a convent and monastery. It was a pretty place set on a lake. I enjoyed the services led by monks who sang hymns in French. I met a sad priest who said he would rather have married and fathered a child. I watched nuns in a small chapel, rosaries hanging from their hands beating against their wombs.

One evening, I made a phone call in a small vestibule of the convent, and a heavy door slammed behind me like the portal to hell. I telephoned my mother who told me my cousin K—— had been killed by a truck on Yonge St. in Toronto. I imagined her body, limp and broken as a martyr's.

Mother Superior cursed me when I knocked to return to my cell. I did not understand her tongue.

The next morning, I found a scrap of paper beneath my door written in the Sister's tight French script. It said I had broken curfew when I used the telephone the night before, and perhaps the convent was not appropriate for me.

As I packed my bag, I asked Jesus to bless my cousin's broken spirit and my own: all that Christianity.

November 26, 2018
Slow Release

Today, I clear belongings from cupboards with the hope that I can change the flow of energy in my small room. The Chinese call this feng shui, an ancient belief that the way your house is built, or you arrange objects, affects your success, health and happiness. It claims to use energy forces to harmonize individuals with their surrounding environment. The term feng shui literally translates as "wind and water" in English, as the feng shui practice also applies to architecture and claims that natural forces bind the Universe, Earth, and humanity together. This is known as qi (pronounced "chee" in English), a positive or negative life force. In feng shui, as in Chinese martial arts, it is energy.

Historically, feng shui was widely used in the design of significant structures such as tombs and other spiritual dwellings. Depending on the style of feng shui employed, an auspicious construction site would be determined by local features such as bodies of water, the slope of the land, vegetation and soil quality. Climates, stars and points on the compass were also considered. In this way, feng shui could be understood as a form of divination that assesses the quality of the local environment and the effects of geography and weather.

Today, feng shui practitioners often work with architects, interior designers and home decorators to maximize the flow of positive energy in an environment. I have hauled four garbage bags to the dumpster and am not finished. I hope that qi is soon released from its bondage.

November 27, 2018
Midnight Clear

I am still clearing my room and smudged it with sage I bought at a Christmas bazaar recently.

Smudging is a spiritual ritual now common among those who practice feng shui. It is also central to many First Nations traditions and alternative healing practices. It involves burning herbs or other natural materials to clear negative energy from a home or space. Smudging is an ancient and sacred ceremony, so I performed it in a slow and mindful manner. I held the bundle over a bowl to prevent embers from falling on the floor. I used a large feather to pass the smoke over my belongings and body, as you can also use smudging to cleanse your own energy.

I opened my bedroom window to allow the darkness to escape like a thief in the night.

November 28, 2018
Roots

I hear spirits, see faces in my glass. Their eyes blue with fatigue. And the Lord comes too. He is crawling God. His knees are bruised. His hands slivered.

I am troubled. I take the pink pills from the cupboard. My heart is an organ, and it plays a sad tune. Spirits come again when my mother leaves the room. They pull faces at her, toss their wigs: strands long and wild as roots.

The Moon is pale and slow in slippers and a bathrobe. She presses her soft cheeks to my breast. I hold her in my flannel arms. She is full and depressed.

I am an old soul. I date from the time of cave. Gathered flowers by a fresh stream. Made love in their wake.

I was growling dog. I was Chinese. I was Native, bloody with pox. I was the wide hips of many women. More sinned against than sinning.

November 29, 2018
Golden Rules

In astrology, a Saturn return occurs when this planet returns to the same place in the sky that it occupied at the time of our birth. While it may not reach the exact spot until we are 29 or 30 years old, its influence is considered to start around age 27. The first orbit is seen as a cosmic rite of passage, of reaching maturity and being faced, perhaps for the first time, with adult challenges and responsibilities. Saturn is the tough taskmaster who tests us and asks us to meet goals.

In my case, I lived alone in Toronto at this time. It was as though I shared my apartment with a life coach who demanded a rigorous psychological and spiritual workout. My astrologer told me that angels and demons were literally battling over my spirit. I was soul weary. I moved to Windsor, Ontario with the hope of kickstarting a new life, but I encountered new challenges there. I met people I likely knew in past lives and felt as though I was a fly caught in a sticky karmic web. One family spun a trap that left me hanging like a helpless insect. When I pulled out of the spidery den, it was as though my tender body had been dismembered. My wings were clipped. But I crossed over this major threshold and entered a new stage of my life.

The return of this planet is scheduled to enter my chart next year and again in my mid 80s, as it takes roughly 30 years for Saturn to orbit the sun. I am anticipating significant changes and patterns. I only pray I am not trapped inside one of its many gold rings.

November 30, 2018
Down

I rest now in soft sheets and a feather tick. How weak I am today. Outside, the earth is soft with late autumn rain.

Remember how I coaxed you, love, into the damp cave of my body? Echo of your proper name. Today, I hear it still inside myself like a bird in a bone cage.

December 1, 2018
Khan Artist

At a recent Cambridge Writers Collective meeting, we selected images of famous historical figures and tried to guess their identities. Mine was an ancient Asian man who wore an earring and a goatee. I described him as an emperor. Later, I discovered he was Genghis Khan (1162 –1227), the founder and first Great Khan of the Mongol Empire, which became the largest continuous empire in history after his death. Genghis Khan grew up in an area dominated by constantly warring clans on the border of modern-day Siberia and Mongolia. He was born into an unstable home and community. His mother had been kidnapped and forced into marriage by his father, a practice in which Genghis Khan himself would later engage. As a child, his father was poisoned and killed by an opposing clan. Genghis Khan got his first taste for blood when he killed his older half-brother to become the dominant male of the family.

He eventually developed a unique strategy for acquiring power. Instead of appointing family or clan members to powerful positions, which was the typical political strategy, he chose allies from other clans or nomadic tribes of Northeast Asia to assist him in his conquests. He and his men would kill the heads of clans then force the survivors to join their united "super-clans." As a result of these invasions and large-scale massacres of civilian populations, Khan conquered most of Eurasia and united previously warring communities. Khan was able to repeat his strategies until he had conquered half the known world and ruled over 1,000,000 people. He governed the areas of modern-day China, Iran, Pakistan, Korea and South Russia. At the height of his conquest, he controlled a land area the size of the continent of Africa. As a result, Genghis Khan was known for the brutality of his campaigns and is considered by many to have been a genocidal ruler. However, he is also credited with bringing the Silk Road under one political environment. This brought relatively easy communication and trade between Northeast Asia, Muslim Southwest Asia, and Christian Europe, expanding the cultural horizons of all three areas. This empire was led by his direct descendants for hundreds of years more, though it gradually broke off into smaller entities over time.

When he conquered a new clan or people, Genghis Khan would force marriage upon the women, either to himself or to his head chiefs. Khan was known to have fathered many children with different women. After conquering a territory, he would choose his pick to add to his harem. Some estimates suggest he impregnated over 1,000 women. As a result, Genghis Khan ranks first for male with the most children in history. Having so many children helped to expand his genetic legacy across the continent. The heirs to Genghis Khan were also prolific. One of his children was thought to have had 40 sons of his own by wives and concubines, with an unknown number of children from many other women. Genghis Khan, himself, died in 1227 at the age of 65 during a battle with a Chinese kingdom, but a study in 2003 found that up to 16 million men, half a percent of the world's male population, were his genetic descendants.

December 2, 2018
Baked Potato

The sticky web of your lives. How you trapped your wives. I feared I too might hang from a strand like a beautiful bug. But I was a young woman, a tuber root. My feet grounded, my energy low. Still, when you touched me dirty in the dark, I worried a child might grow in me like a potato.

December 3, 2018
Shang Dynasty

I wrote a poem that placed in a mystical writing contest. I believe I am an old soul who lived mostly in China. I imagine in the poem that I was dying in another life and that spirits came to usher me into the next world. It was a dreamy time, and I saw a red bird whose feathers represented my many incarnations. She was also a symbol of love, sent by the Emperor who offered prayers to gods in the temple above. The piece is called "Shang Dynasty" which is the era believed to be responsible for the foundations of Chinese culture and civilization:

Shang Dynasty

In the days
before I passed,
spirits came, their hands
great with blooms.
But they did not bear
the red bird of China,
its scarlet plumes.

In dreams,
the Emperor
offered prayers
in the Temple of Heaven.

And outside, the bird
rested on my shoulder:
a harbinger of love.
Wings wide,
feathers like past lives
red as blood.

December 3, 2018
Festival of Lights

I once loved a Jewish fellow and wrote this poem for him. Today is the first day of Hanukkah and so retrieved this piece again from a journal entry:

Imagine I am your wife.
I have knit a shawl.
Touched your yarmulke
on the Shabbat
at sun fall.

But you don't love me
though I polish
the menorah
wear a wig
recite a Hebrew prayer
begat sons and daughters.

But we light the Hannukah candles
eight days, celebrate
the miracle of holy oil
in the temple.
Your mystical eyes
yellow as flames.

December 4, 2018
Rain in the Desert

I wondered when I wrote this poem whether parts of the Earth and Mother Nature sin when they do not offer us opportunity for natural growth or viable life. I believe the globe is a living being who resists supporting us in various parts of the world like deserts and frozen tundra. I imagine it holds memory of cultures who have attempted to survive in these difficult environments.

Archaeology
The Lord lifts
a wafer
in His dirty hands.
The Lord, who prepared
the dry earth,
kneels upon
its darkness:
its past lives
and its sins.

December 5, 2018
Temptation

I wrote a little piece in a writing workshop a couple of years ago and found it among my papers recently. It is a fictional account of a boy who is sexually abused. I imagined him so hurt that he suffers a crisis of faith that lasts into adulthood. I hope it serves as a statement to those who are tempted to seduce children:

Crisis of Faith

Sally woke me with a cup of dark brew. I drank it slow in the soft sheets. Showered and shaved, snapped my partial plate in place.

Sally answered a steady knock at the door. My dog, Homer, barked. It was Guy, our postman, with a pink envelope. I opened it with caution for the return address was Squashville. The letter was typed and signed by a Gloria Hunty, personal support worker to my grandfather Lane. I read it quickly, though my heart waned.

•

I passed Lil's Variety and St. John's on the Hill, fields of autumn corn. The new moon was low. I was weary, so stopped my van at Ruby's Good Eats. I ordered a cup of coffee and a piece of raisin pie. I wiped a bit of crust from the corner of my moustache, then the bell on the door rang: Terrence LaValley slid by. He was tanned and leathery and wore a flannel shirt. It was red and had seen better days. His jeans were worn at the knees, his work boots muddy. He nodded toward me, for I have aged gracefully despite my teeth. I remember his dirty touch one evening. I was a child among the sheaves.

•

My grandfather passed a few hours before. Gloria Hunty pulled a sheet over the corpse. I remembered his white cane. How he tapped among the fields near Terrence LaValley: his wink and his pocketknife. The moon a white pool that night. But the Lord, like Lane, turned a blind eye. He stumbled in the dark with His guide dog and His wife and Their disabled son Christ.

December 6, 2018
Christ Mass

I am interested in women who bear children and who reflect upon the process in a Christian context.

Risen Lord

Bless her mound
ripened round as a moon
or a fruit
gathering silent
in a womb of time.

Babe's heart a tiny cup
for blood.
Yours, Lord, a wafer,
a broken host.
Given for her.
All that love.

The blanket is pink.
Babe's breath rises and falls
like a dove.

It sets on Mama's breast.

Mama sings a hymn:
Jesus crucified,
his soft belly
great with egg.

December 7, 2018
Soul Mating

I am a romantic who wonders why the object of my affection still resists me:

Come C—, my love.
I imagine the way you touch:
your hands are soft
as doves.
They rest on the perch
of my bosom
set in the hollow
of my throat.
Our hearts —
their steady beats —
coo in the dark.

December 8, 2018
Writer's Block

I discovered a series of fictional prose poems in a drawer today. I wrote it when I was studying toward my Master's degree in creative writing in Montreal over 30 years ago.

The Blue Angel

Minnie

I saw Jake at the Angel. He hadn't shaved in a week, and I could smell him from across the table. Told me he's learned to juggle and can play *La Vie en Rose* on his fiddle now.

I know it was not Jake Lizzy desired. She could not bear that another knew my scent, my command of pillows and the old iron bed.

It wasn't the first time. There was Bennett who brought over hot dogs, mustard and tall beers. He delivered dinner in a wicker basket. I liked him. Lizzy shuffled around the living room in his boots, fingered the wallet he'd taken from his pants pocket. Even read the letter I had written, and he hid inside the soft leather folds.

These days I am alone, though I saw Lizzy in a bookstore. I cowered in the gardening section. She wore black gauze. Her bangs were moist with heat. She was expecting a child. I crouched among the roses.

Last week, I dreamed I delivered her baby in an old shack. I was the midwife who pulled it feet first from her open legs. Her son screamed to leave her bloody warmth and rest in her bony arms. I knew he was the son of Jake. I christened him Earlock: he would not hush.

Jake

Good to seen Minnie at the Angel, but I liked her hair long. My roommate, Hank, wears two braids like an Indian. I say, 'right on.'

I liked Lizzie better than Minnie, true. Dark curls and eyes and the way she'd twist her hips. Called me wily coyote. I never liked those round cheeks of Minnie's, the way her chin doubles.

I think of Lizzie when I smoke my clay pipe or sometimes over thick coffee. Once I took her to the Blue Angel. We didn't need no love-magic prescription. She sung me hurtin' songs, and later I lifted her flowered skirts and made like a coydog, cunnin' and wild. Drove Lizzy to howl.

Lizzy

The midwife was a handsome woman, though she had a beaked nose. I called to God when it hurt bad. He told me to raise the boy alone. It was born without eyebrows, a line of hair on its ears. I cursed Jake.

I think of Minnie, still, her moist hands, big shoes, eyes.

Jewel

Minnie grabbed my knee when he came into the Angel. I never seen the man, didn't know what got into her. His name was Jake, she said. I was talkin' to my pal Elvis who got a pair a cool rockabilly shoes. I was tellin' him I sold a earrings and matchin' necklace set to Stompin Tom's wife. Then Minnie tweaked my leg. I gave her a cigarette and got her singin' "I Fall to Pieces." Molly at the guitar thought Minnie sang good.

Lizzy

The hairs have fallen from his ears, and there are fine eyebrows sprouting. Still, he is Jake's thing and I won't be telling him.

When Minnie dragged home that hillbilly, I had to make like I was wild for him, so he wouldn't leave little bruises on my angel's neck.

Minnie made me pretty. She was like a grandie flower at the bosom of a party frock, a coney fur collar on a plain broadcloth coat, a princess slip — lingerie of rare loveliness.

Lizzy

Bathtub, cradle, rattle, suck.

Kid likes strained peaches in a dish.

I hold him late night. Open nightgown: breast.

But world outside like a lit birthday cake. I take a breath.

Minnie

I'm afraid to wear my birthstones. In dreams I turn my rubies to my palms, make fists and punch. But the red jewels bleed down my wrists.

Jewel

Minnie and I talk like a couple a church wives Monday nights.

Like the angel, saint of our drinkin' hole, Minnie's a bit blue.

Minnie's big mistake was she thought Jake and Lizzie worth stringin' and wearin' close to her heart. I could tell to look at them they wasn't no gems, not even bobbles. But Minnie's a beaut.

Rain Man

This poem was written years ago when my father's passing was still fresh.

I imagined he might break from a cloud.

Shuttles

The warp and weft
of the days.
God's loom:
blue fabric bloomed.

But I prayed for my late father
to fall from the seam
of a threadbare cloud
torn as soft cloth.

I dreamed of a heavy drape
of rain.
My father drenched to the bone.

December 10, 2018

Israel

My gown is dusk.
My body a tell:
when I offered myself
to Christians and their horses
2,000,000 Crusaders and Muslims
died against my bosom.

December 12, 2018
Hunger Pains

For a couple of years, I volunteered at the local foodbank. I worked in the emergency grocery store distributing provisions to needy people and their children. I envisioned a very-different model: a warehouse where families could serve themselves and shop for mostly canned goods like Chunky Soup and stew. I would dispense with paperwork and red tape and would open the doors to those who required our support. I believe these hungry people would take only what they needed and could carry. My foodbank would operate on an honour system.

Foodbank

The hungry come to me
bearing open bags
and empty babes.
Their first word
not Mama or Love
but Empty —
as a trapped dove
in a cage of bone.
Its scaly feet tied
with a strip of rag.
Its soft body trussed
with cloth.
Even its cry
a gagged song.

December 13, 2018
Animal Crackers

These poems reflect stories a spiritual friend told me. They allude to her childhood and sexual abuse she suffered at the hand of her father. He was a crude man, an animal who scarred her innocence and her love of self.

Dog Bones

Lay it down.
His soul like a wild dog.
His thing soft then stiff.
A burnt cigarette in his paw.
How to say
we rested
though in dreams something howled.

Blossoms of blood.
I was broken and barefoot.
My dress a rag.

Then the hound dead.
Buried under a stone.
A daisy on the heap.
A sweet-smelling woman
wished him deep sleep.
She is my mother.
She balanced by a river
and prayed his soul
the Lord to keep.
Alone in her grief.

Burial Rites

The earth where a horse rests.
A stone heavy
and beneath bones and teeth.

I have hung his bridle
in the barn.

I was a child
balanced on a great beast.
My innocent thighs open.

I think now of the man
buried too.
It is the morning of the moon.
He is risen.

December 14, 2018
United Church

I am cat sitting for S— who suffers from schizophrenia. There is evidence in her small apartment that she has tried to heal her troubled mind with Christ. I leaf through a book called *A Melody of Love*. It is a challenge to be a fundamentalist Christian even for a healthy person, I think to myself. "Live in harmony by showing love for each other. Be united in what you think, as if you were only one person" wrote Paul to the Philippians (2:2). I don't understand how minds can unite, especially those inherently sick. I imagine a world where there is only one opinion, one belief, one culture. I imagine one gender, one race, one sexual orientation. Diversity has been the hallmark of this world since the dawn of time, I think. To homogenize our thought processes would not be possible without divine intervention and even so would take generations to achieve.

In the case of my friend, her mind haunts her with voices, chants, whispers and screams. It tells her she will die soon and go to hell. She has not been healed despite attempts at committing to various faiths, rituals and religious practices. Perhaps the Lord is unable to repair the damage with which she incarnated. As a result, I doubt He could unite thoughts, as Paul claimed.

I love the idea of a Messiah who might lay his hands on my friend's head, sickness like a small bird trembling. But I have difficulty with scripture, dogma and religious tracts. Instead, I praise small moments.

December 15, 2018
Visionary

I wrote my cousin A— a poem many years ago. She was losing her sight at the time, and I mourned. I composed the piece in dialect, as I love writers like William Faulkner and John Steinbeck who capture the rhythm, cadence and quirky language of southern Americans.

My cousin A— is a very-talented Canadian and now famous in some circles. She is a playwright, screenwriter, actor, theatre director, teacher, singer and songwriter. She had been interviewed on CBC radio and on television, profiled by newspapers like the *Toronto Star*. Last Christmas, she starred in a play produced in Toronto called *The Story* that was staged outdoors. She has won many prestigious awards and been recognized as an advocate for disabled people. Cousin A— has also travelled all over the world and lived for years alone in London, England where she worked in theatre. She is a slim woman but strong in spirit. Her big laugh resonates in my mind when I am low or weak. I imagine her lighting my dark days.

Cousin

She doesn't see good; she got a eye thing. It's like spiders in the blue part, or when the moon draws itself over the sun.

When Cousin and me go out, I hold her in the crook of her arm, I tell her when the sprinkler's going to spit, when to step down and if the light says green.

Sometimes we go for coffee. She takes hers black, so I don't tell about the sugar and about the pitcher of cream. We like to sit at the booth in the back 'cause we got secrets. Cousin's got a big voice, and she laughs deep, but I know there is a cry in her, it's wet and runs wide like a puddle. There is a cry in me, too.

Today, a man on the bus, he got big sad eyes. His shirt got a print of wild birds: ostriches in stride, woodpeckers, their beaks. A sparrow's nest. He makes a gun with his finger and points it at a puff of red feathers where his heart beats. I don't tell Cousin about the man. And I don't tell about the robin's tender breast.

December 16, 2018
Face Lift

A little poem about the explorer Ponce de León who some say travelled from Spain to Florida in search of a Fountain of Youth in the year 1514. I imagine him as a dreamy fellow prone to fantasy, yearning for a pool of healing waters to rinse age and sickness from the countenance and body. I wish I had access to such a fountain. It might wash the highs and lows from my face like spiritual Oil of Olay.

Ponce de León

At night, in the hull of the ship
he dreams of the Fountain of Youth
in the mythical land of Bimini.
His body, a new root, blooms.
His face soft as orchid.
The waters wash the blue
from his heart:
a bulb, fertile and sacred.

December 17, 2018
Original Sin

This poem reflects my concern for the abuse many Aboriginal women have suffered throughout history. I worked with Native men in a local jail one summer. They were incarcerated for violence against women. I brought them healing herbs I hoped might cleanse their spirits.

This poem, however, is about a White fellow in the Depression era who abandons his Indian gal. I wrote it as an exercise one night at the Cambridge Writers Collective. We were to develop a character we had already created in previous work. My woman first appeared in my book *A Salve For Every Sore*. Her name is Spotted Calf.

Brown Eggs

White lover traded me
for spoons and socks
and a sack of sugar.
"Because it was rain
in the desert," he said.

"You sure is pretty, though," he added.
"Your skin the shade of brown eggs
and your hair long and straight
as twine."

I am woman
made by the Creator.
My heart husked like corn
and my girl-part too
sensitive as fruit.
I will peel it
for a good man
and make a babe.

I will carry her
in a soft suede bag
lined in fallen leaves.
Always loose
and gently laid.

December 18, 2018
Clean Bill of Health

I believe that oral health and basic hygiene are key to a healthy spirituality. I love toiletries, shampoos and pastes. I feel they allow us to thank God for the gift of incarnation and permit us to honour the divine with a clean body and face. When I was a child, I gave my father a Christmas gift, a white soap called Pope on a Rope.

December 19, 2018
'Canon'balls

I am interested in recovering women's stories from the Biblical texts. I read them from a feminist perspective and mine them for evidence that might support those principles. I believe that many are evidence of the cultures and faith communities that developed them and are entwined with their mores and beliefs. Stories about God and women are always mediated through shifting historical discourse. Tracing these changes both in the scriptural period and subsequent history makes it clear that discussion about women is always tied to cultural contexts. The Second Vatican Council even spoke of this by using the organic metaphor of growth.

I take this premise a step further. I believe in an open canon (which is derived from the Greek word meaning 'rule' or 'measuring stick') that would include continuous revelation: reinterpretations of stories, related experience and historically relevant documents. This would allow for an open-ended talk about God and women. It would also allow for contributions from women such as Sallie McFague who attempt to makes use of metaphor to conceive of women and God, though no language is adequate or proper, she says.

It is true, that an open-ended Bible would be difficult to regulate and physically cumbersome to store. A canonical panel would need to be established to adjudicate submissions. Another option might be a call for relevant works, documents, stories and poems by female and male authors which would not be physically bound to the scriptures but would be used in sermons and academic works and at religious gatherings.

Human experience has become an identifying feature of many contemporary theologies. Contemporary beliefs, experiences and techniques should be applied to the ancient Biblical texts to uncover new meanings and to support women who are sometimes still blamed for ancient sins and weakness and limited to bringing forth sons for men.

Moreover, we require new insights because the story of Christianity is always told from a male point of view by the Gospel writers, and the creative reflection and participation of women is neglected or marginalized. If Church leaders do not include writings from contemporary women in their sermons and talks, Christians will continue to repeat metaphors for God and Jesus in the language of ruling men. The words and interpretations of the Bible are not written in stone. They are subject to new forms of expression and scripting. For instance, much anguish and debate in the 19th century led to texts in the Bible that supported slavery to be laid aside. It was agreed that they did not contribute to the good news of Christianity but sustained a genuinely evil social institution. The same dynamic now directs the interpretation of patriarchal or sexist Biblical texts: whether they offer salvation for the most abused of women.

December 21, 2018
God on High

As a child, I invited Jesus into the pool of my heart, but he could not balance there, for my father's sickness drew the living waters from me. My father's illness was a tide. There were high or manic periods when I could not bear the shame: a public display beneath the hilltop church of my baptism, late night rants and verbal threats, large-scale purchases and odd equipment.

Unwittingly, my father invoked in me the god of the Israelites: a capricious and punitive deity whose emotional outbursts I could not appease through sacrifice or good works. Like the Psalmist David, I prayed,

O Lord, do not rebuke me in

your anger,
or discipline me in your wrath.
(Psalm 6)

My father's intense moods determined the emotional conditions of my small world and the nature of my relationship with Yahweh, a god who like my father, had a flair for the dramatic but whose responses were mounted on a large-scale stage:

The crash of your thunder was in
the whirlwind;
your lightnings lit up the world;
the earth trembled and shook.
(Psalm 77)

At the same time, my father displayed qualities which I loved and which I could not reconcile with the vicious man who, at times, treated my mother and me with such cruelty. This man of gentle action and of rage.

The religion to which I was introduced as a child brought me little comfort or relief. It was a bland form of Anglicanism taught to me at a suburban Toronto church I attended with my mother. I learned the basic principles and tenets of Christianity in confirmation classes there and even asked Jesus into my heart one night in the shadows of my canopy. But I learned more from simply sitting beside my mother in a pew. Hers was a simple faith that did not rely on sophisticated theological pondering. She had little relationship to the concepts of sin and salvation or incarnate Word. She prayed to God on a regular basis, and she was kind.

But my mother never forgot the day she disclosed my father's illness to our minister. He dropped by the house unexpectedly while my father was away on business. She described the symptoms and effects of his manic depression. "God is testing you," the Reverend said. This was his theological understanding of illness, suffering and trial. It was a response that left my mother feeling unsupported and alienated from both her church and her God. The minister's pastoral visit also led her to believe that there was a solidarity between my father and him. They had once exchanged the Masonic handshake, my mother later learned, and in doing so established a masculine bond that seemed to exclude her.

As a woman, I later fell in love with a man who had devoted his life to the Problem of Evil. Perhaps my inner child recalled the minister's feeble explanation of the pain my father's illness had caused. Perhaps I wed myself to a spiritual solution to the early confusion and to the moral issues it raised for me.

Unfortunately, as I grew close to this man the strength of his persona dissolved. He was also unstable, unreliable and immoral. He translated his belief that freedom is the source of human suffering into a personal misuse of power and emotional manipulation.

My wedding gown and veil now hang in a closet. I came dangerously close to wearing that gauze of deception, that flimsy understanding of God and of relationship and of love.

I have since centred myself in a syncretism of High Anglicanism, astrology, feminist and process theologies, paganism, Buddhism, and New Age spirituality. It is a blend that reflects my old soul and my personal and mystical experiences. Recently, a colleague who is not religious, said my poetry appealed to her because it is "universal."

But when I was 28, I registered for the Master of Divinity program at Trinity College. It was a decision that evolved out of religious imagery in dreams, my encounter with Father M—, who taught at the university, and lack of a clear direction at the time. I enrolled in the "non-ordination" stream, but unfortunately was unable to maintain my syncretic vision in that environment. While a few of my male peers seemed to find me charming, they imposed their rational and rigid theologies upon my intuitive understandings. The Chaplain suggested that I pack my tarot cards, books, and tokens in a shoe box and that he hide it somewhere at Trinity College. He jokingly called it Pandora's box.

In an ironic reversal of the Greek myth, the sealing of Pandora's box resulted in the release of many dark and destructive forces and impulses in my life. I left the M.Div program in October of my second year and spent the next few in a debilitating depression that prevented me from working. The disabling symptoms of this illness included anxiety attacks and a sense of alienation from God.

My recovery was slow but was aided by medication, exercise and ultimately by enrolling in an M.A. program in religious studies at the University of Windsor. There I was exposed to a variety of religious traditions, as well as feminist and other contemporary theologies. When I was ill, I believed that I would always live in silence, my body an abandoned convent haunted by quiet Sisters. But soon I began to hear a voice that help define my spirituality, values and decisions, and to shape my poetry and short stories. My little book *The Weight of Wings* stuttered from me. It was a title that seemed to capture the tension between the slow drag of my body at the time and my spiritual objectives. I wrote some of the poems in that collection on my hands and knees. Crawling God and the spirits of the wounded knelt there with me.

The book was not well distributed, but a professor in the department of Religion and Culture at Wilfrid Laurier University added it to the curriculum of a course called Women's Lives and Religious Values. It was also nominated for the Pat Lowther Memorial Award for the best book of poetry by a Canadian woman. Pat Lowther was a Canadian poet who was murdered by her husband about 40 years ago. I did not win the prize, but shortly before the adjudication I dreamed that Pat Lowther made me a pot of tea.

December 24, 2018
Handmaid's Tale

My attempt at an alternative Marian Christmas poem:

Christmas

The winter sun.
Midwives, my thighs.
My belly a shrine.
He breaks from me
like a turtledove.
He is made of bone and blood.
The women sing hymns
wash him in a shallow tub.
He is damp in cloth
his hair bears the shine of feathers.
My breasts blossom
with the light of his mouth.

This night, Goddess, too,
bears a weight — of moon.

December 25, 2018

Scar Tissue

I am the only child.
A small worry
born of a scar.
Come, Jesus
for you are Lord of wounds.
I am a sad prayer
my father spoke in tongues.
I am a wishbone
my mother broke
in her tired hands.

His Body

We wash the Lord.
His sensitive hair.
Rinse it in chamomile and moon.
He is of the clean morning.

We have come to him.
His eyes are seeds.

We are his people
his blooms.

December 27, 2018

Timepiece

My spirit is alone,
but trips a wedding march.

For you are all that is:
blood, a pot of rosehip tea,
a fallen apple-tree
its rough bark...

Your heart
is a used wristwatch
those dirty hands.

But I am a woman
breathing time.
I will make everything
to all of you.
I will pant.

For I am a moment
unfolding like a clock
the sound of a god
making love.

December 27, 2018
Body and Sole

Last night I dreamed of Father W——. He returned to our Anglican Divinity school (where I trained for a year, and he was ordained) from New

York where he led a children's choir school. I was over the moon to see him again. We left the school and headed into some woods where there were shoe stores. He tried on boots which I felt were a bit puffy and kind of nerdy looking. Then he stumbled upon a pair of black sandals that were unique because they featured double soles that were detachable. I called them "theological shoes." What could this nifty footwear suggest symbolically, I asked myself when I woke. A little research suggested that a dream about shoes may symbolize moving forward on a career or spiritual path in life. A change of shoes may represent a major change in life, such as job, relationship or even attitude. Considering these possibilities, I think my former friend's new footwear is a symbol of my own journey, since it appeared in my dream. Perhaps I am finally wearing my own spirituality: a two-tiered approach to both Christianity and the powers of nature (for the shoe stores, as I say, were located in a forest). I can only pray that Father W's— double soles will be worn by others too and that many of us will walk in the comfort of these new shoes.

December 28, 2018
Baby

Many people in my life call me Baby.

Baby Talk

I am Baby:
my heart was a turtle
learning to crawl.
The soft underbelly
a shadow beneath its shell.

Flowerchild

I heard the Demon
clear his dirty throat.

My breasts were soft orchids
where he lived
like an infant
sucking my milk.
Cry Baby

Demon, today my body is a weak sapling. You tear at my roots, course through my limbs like a bitter sap. My hands are old leaves.

Hoodoo Man

My lover is close
though he has passed.

How to see ghosts?
Break a rain-crow egg
into water and wash
your face.
Harness the moon.

His hair is plaited long.
He sings me cradle songs.

I am Baby
prone to tears.
He tells me,
"Be tender to your dream-soul
for it is bruised."

In the morning
dust on the mirror.

December 30, 2018
Blind Love

In this poem, I imagine a disabled man who expresses himself through his sexuality. The narrator is a woman who pines for his former affections. I placed them in a rural environment among peasants who love in colourful and sensuous settings.

Skin and Bone

It was the hour of the moon
and peasants sang their love songs
peeled the skins of oranges
and took persimmons in their dry hands.
My lover was in the hills
with a lean woman
smoke on their lips.

I walked the iron rails
where corn rustles like skirts.
Remembered how lover traced my body
in the dirt.

Days now in the root cellar
where it is cool:
baskets of potatoes and yams.
I hold them like talismans
divine their eyes.

Lover might bear me
stones and bones.
Leave his woman.
Lover's eyes are muddy pools
his hands bleed with small sores.
His tongue is a swollen root.
But he might touch me
as a peasant fondles fruit.

January 2, 2019
Voice Lessons

Three little poems written when I was a teenager. They are not thematically linked. Simply a few examples of fictional verse from the 1980s, when I was struggling to find my poetic voice:

Down-to-there pearls
and forget-me-not gown
I cha-cha in the garden
throwing my hips
against the night
reaching long and hanging
oh-so-glamorous
like a dropped earring
sapphire against
the moon's powdered face.

On our Sunday evening strolls
Grandmother Ruby wore her hat
with the veil.

Behind the net
her eyes two fishes
glowing blue
in the pink night.

Chatting we walked
hand in hand
me dressed in Granny's beads
big as snails.

Sunday, years later
cleaning out a drawer
I find the strand
beached at the bottom.
Against my ear
they are silent as Ruby.

Mama lies like a question mark
beside me.
My sleeve still damp
from scrubbing.
Clothesline above us:
my nightie, her slip
hand-soap clean.
Ghostly and quivering
from January's breath.

January 3, 2019
Evil Eye

My close friend L— gifted me with treasures she purchased on her Mediterranean cruise this Christmas. I am intrigued by a small glass talisman from Greece called an "evil eye" and thought to protect a person from a curse (also called the evil eye, or mati in Greek) given by a glare that causes misfortune or injury. These malevolent looks are usually given to a person when they are unaware. In fact, any negative emotion is believed to cause the evil eye curse such as anger or jealousy and can result in headaches or a string of bad luck. Wearing the charm is said to help prevent the curse from even happening. Belief in the evil eye dates to Classical antiquity, and more than one hundred works by authors such as Plato and Alexander the Great mention the evil eye. In the Aegean Region, people with green and especially blue eyes are relatively rare and are thought to bestow the curse, intentionally or unintentionally. Thus, in Greece and Turkey amulets like mine take the form of a big blue eye. In Santorini, Greece, one of the most beautiful, luxurious and popular islands of the world, L— said roofs are painted blue to prevent evil. I intend to purchase a long leather rope for my charm and wear it around my neck. I hope it will reduce the recurring headaches I have suffered lately, cast an intimidating stare from the lid of my heart.

January 4, 2019
Audrey Hepburn

I share a birthday, May 4th, with actress Audrey Hepburn and have always felt a kinship with this fellow Taurus. I admire her charm, beauty, grace, elegance, talent and philanthropy. And, of course, the vulnerability of her lovely swan neck. I was excited, too, to learn recently that like me, Audrey owned a Yorkshire Terrier. He was called Mr. Famous. He appeared as the dog in the basket during the train shot of the film *Anna Karenina*. Audrey and I also share a love of gardens and the living art of flowers. This interest helped influence her decision to host a documentary series, *Gardens of the World*, which aired in 1993, shortly after her death. But Audrey Hepburn was best known as one of Hollywood's greatest style icons and actors — one of the few to win an Emmy, Tony, Grammy, and Academy Award.

Audrey's acting, however, took a back seat to her work on behalf of children. She was named a goodwill ambassador for UNICEF in the late 1980s. She travelled the world, making more than 50 trips, raising awareness about children in need in Asia, Africa and Central and South America. Audrey understood what it was like to go hungry from her days as a child in The Netherlands during the German Occupation. She won a special Academy Award for her humanitarian work in 1993, but she did not live long enough to receive it. Audrey died at her home in Switzerland after a battle with appendiceal cancer. Later, UNICEF honoured Audrey Hepburn's legacy of humanitarian work by unveiling a statue, "The Spirit of Audrey," at UNICEF's New York headquarters. Her service for children is also recognized through an American UNICEF fund.

Since Audrey's passing, her grave site in Switzerland is one of the biggest tourist attractions throughout Europe. It garners hundreds of thousands of people from all over the world. For Audrey Hepburn made a total of 31 high-quality movies. Her elegance and style will always be remembered in film history: she was named in *Empire* magazine's "The Top 100 Movie Stars of All Time." She was also on the cover of *Life* magazine nine times, more than any other celebrity. In 1954, *Vogue* magazine wrote that she had established a new "standard of beauty."

January 5, 2019
Heart Strings

When D— became engaged to a professional violinist who played for Celine Dion and other famous vocalists, she asked me to be one of her bridesmaids. We had been close friends in Montreal where I studied creative writing and she film. She was a lovely-looking young woman —

very-long wavy red hair, big brown eyes, and porcelain skin. She was tall and slim like a ballet dancer. Her short films were rich in texture and tapestry, reflecting her Hungarian roots. Her father had emigrated from that country many years before and was a practicing neurosurgeon and professor. Her mother was a nurse.

But artistic talent dripped from D's— long, narrow hands. She often wore purple and pearls, and in the winter a large mutton coat she draped with scarves. I wrote a rhythmic chant for a film she made. I think that it reflected the cries in the woman's mind and the imagery of the piece.

D's— beau was a fully-bilingual fellow from the Eastern Townships of Quebec. He had lost most of his hair prematurely, but D— delighted in his bald pate and rubbed it regularly, calling him simply "Egg." When he proposed to her, he offered her a gold ring adorned with a purple stone, and she accepted.

I had a dress made for the occasion of taupe-coloured shot-silk and her younger sister wore the same fabric in a burnt-orange shade. We shared a room at Manoir Hovey on the shores of Lake Massawippi in North Hatley. But she never spoke a word to me.

The weather was also cold that January. But I traversed the ice in high-heeled pumps and reached a Roman Catholic church in town called Église de Sainte-Élisabeth. D— had sewn her own wedding gown. It was large, white and puffy. She curled her auburn hair and tied it in thin gold ribbons. She also decorated a pair of high-heeled mules with bows. She looked like a Christmas gift.

The service was in French, but D's— older sister P— who lived in Paris, France whispered translations to me in English. We sat in a front pew. "Some people are meant to be together, the priest says," she told me.

Later, at the reception, we smoked cigarettes and whispered about P—'s man who was expected to fly in from France at any time. He was a large Black fellow, originally from Cameroon and who was raised in a mud hut. His grandmother was a witch doctor. He never appeared at the wedding, and later she learned he was still in Paris, dying of bone cancer, despite a vaccination from the tongue of a viper his grandmother once administered in Africa.

I was asked to write a poem for the occasion of D—'s wedding. It was a piece about frequent pots of tea D— and I shared in my apartment on Lambert Closse in Montreal. She was a Gemini and talked quickly, lighting on subject after subject like a bird might land on hydro wire. I was so nervous before her friends and family my hands flapped like the few leaves still clinging to trees outside the inn. Nevertheless, it proved to be a popular prose poem that has since been published a few times.

On leaving the celebration, a group of us piled into a car, and it slid dangerously close to the edge of a precipice. Shrubs were cloaked in ice like suits of shining armour. I was bundled in the backseat with D's— half-sister, a successful artist who suffered from schizophrenia. "I need a knife for the ghosts," she said.

When I eventually moved to Cambridge, I continued to hear from D— who became a high-school art teacher and a mother. She sent me a photo of her first child, a boy. He looked like her husband except for his head of fine red hair. I gradually heard less and less from her, and then there was a silence that still stretches from Montreal to southwestern Ontario like a long row of downed telephone poles.

January 6, 2019
Gone with the Wind

Last night, I dreamed of Canadian Poet Laureate John B. Lee who has been instrumental in my career. He was deliberating as to whether to publish a book of all the poems he has ever written, or study towards a Ph.D. on *Gone with the Wind*. I don't have a dream analyst in my life anymore, so don't really know what my unconscious was trying to communicate to me. *Gone with the Wind* was the first and one of the only films I saw with both of my parents at the box office. But some dreams require a little research:

Gone with the Wind is an epic, romantic, historical film based on Margaret Mitchell's sweeping 1936 novel. More than 30 million copies of the Pulitzer Prize winning book have been sold. It is often considered the most beloved and highest-earning film of all time and won 10 Oscars at the 12th Academy Awards ceremony. Moreover, its supporting actress, Hattie McDaniel, became the first African American to win a coveted Academy Award.

I think my dream might mean that I should take the short screenwriting workshop for which I have registered at the end of January seriously. I should try to write a little film. I once took a weekend-long course with Hollywood screenwriter Robert McKee but never pursued what I learned from him.

I have a character in mind. She is a shy, insecure and abused young woman who ultimately speaks her mind. Her name is Beauty. I can only dream she becomes a cultural legend like Margaret Mitchell's Scarlett O'Hara, defending her land and transforming herself into a heroic, strong-willed and spiritual force in a contemporary Canadian drama. Hopefully, audiences will *give a damn!*

January 10, 2019
Body of Christ

Today, I met with my friend S— who suffers from schizophrenia and celiac disease (she is sensitive to gluten found in wheat, rye and barley). She had a donut with her coffee, and I asked if it was gluten-free. She said God had sanctified it, and she would be able to safely digest it.

Little is known about schizophrenia. It seems to me to be a spiritual disorder. I don't doubt that those who suffer with it hear messages from Spirit, but they don't always seem true or beneficial. The spirit world is a busy and deceiving place, I think. Gods, demons, spirits and other entities move in and out of some of us confusing our perception of reality. I imagine the portal of these minds unlocked and the personal rooms there inhabited by divine trespassers. In the case of my friend, I watched her take a bite of the cruller. I wondered if she would receive it like gluten-free holy bread or a sweet med. Would it dissolve on her tongue like the body of Christ or upset her tender tum?

January 14, 2019
Felicity

I enjoy watching tarot-card readings on YouTube in the evenings. Tonight, I have tuned into Felicity's channel. She is an attractive African American. I like her face and her lively predictions for the sign of Taurus in the month of January. I look forward to help from the ancestors, the healing of my broken heart, a blessed union by archangel Uriel. Keys and doors are images that recur...A lion, four coins, the King of Swords. Felicity cracks open a deck I've never seen. It's called Magical Mermaids and Dolphins. "Let go of old guilt, you're God's perfect child," she drawls. "The Treasure Chest! — consult a financial expert, an unforeseen windfall..."

January 17, 2019
Predictions

The morning opens the palm of her hand. I read the blue veins, the mount of Jupiter, the lines like rivers flowing into the hard, white flesh of her land. I divine the bones of winter: limbs of trees fallen in pattern. The Lord will rise again.

January 18, 2019
Cranium

I have had migraine headaches recently: my skull crowned with a heavy weight. I drifted in and out of consciousness. Spirits left me. They were sick, too, touched their heads as though broken bowls, precious porcelain. Fine fissures and lines divined by the demon who spoke the spell.

January 20, 2019
Birthday of the Trees

Tu BiShvat or the "birthday" of all fruit trees is a minor Jewish festival which this year will be celebrated on January 21st. Rituals associated with this holiday could have fallen out of practice after the destruction of the Second Temple in 70 CE, however they were revived by kabbalists (mystics) in the late Middle Ages. Today, participants practice a Tu BiShvat Seder that is modelled on the Passover Seder. The Tu BiShvat Seder includes eating fruits and nuts traditionally associated with the Holy Land and drinking four cups of red and white wine which symbolize various seasons of the year. Selections from Biblical and rabbinic readings are also featured at this celebration. Deuteronomy 8:8, for instance, states there are five fruits and two grains associated with Israel including grapes, figs, dates, olives and pomegranates, wheat and barley. Kabbalists added almonds to the list, as they believed almond trees were the first in Israel to blossom. But today there are many variations in how to prepare a Tu BiShvat meal. It often incorporates dried fruit and nuts. For environmentalists, the occasion is an ancient connection to modern ecological issues and concerns. The holiday is seen as a time to educate Jewish people and other participants about responsible stewardship of creation. The sources of Tu BiShvat celebrate nature, and so it is a time to care for the environment. Since the Jewish tradition has long been sensitive to such issues, it is common to plant trees on this day. In climates where this is not possible, participants will plant parsley seeds. The parsley will then be included on the Passover Seder plate. Many American and European Jews observe the holiday by donating money to the Jewish National Fund, which is devoted to reforesting Israel. Some do this annually in honour of their children.

This year, for the fourth time, a Tu BiShvat Seder will be celebrated as an evening of sharing Jewish and Indigenous nature rituals at a synagogue in Toronto. The Jewish holiday will become a platform for celebrating these cultural traditions through song, poetry, reflections and traditional food. It will be held at Holy Blossom Temple on Bathurst St. and will be facilitated by an Anishinaabe Traditional Teacher and two female rabbis. They will explore Indigenous and Jewish connections to nature. I regret that I cannot participate, as the event is sold out, but today I purchased a package of parsley seeds.

January 20, 2019
Super Blood Wolf Moon

This morning the sun like a pearl in its shell pales compared to the great ruby I imagine on the hand of tonight's night sky: a Super Blood Wolf

Moon. I look forward to this total lunar eclipse, the longest of the 21st century and the last to grace our sky until May 26, 2021.

Just hours after this eclipse there will be an unusual pairing of Venus and Jupiter in the pre-dawn. Anyone in Western Europe will be able to see Venus and Jupiter 'kiss.'

Some astrologers predict that tonight's Super Blood Wolf Moon will intensify the already powerful energies of the full moon and that the effects will linger up to six months after this significant lunar eclipse. This full moon in Leo is already positive, fiery and enthusiastic. The main theme of this eclipse is 'gaining more than we ask for.' Often, we ask for what is realistic, this moon encourages us to know our true potential. We are likely to earn, achieve and manifest under this stunning red orb situated near the border between Cancer and Gemini.

Ancients who studied the skies, often tracked the changing seasons by studying the lunar month rather than the solar year, upon which the 12 months in our modern calendar are based. It seems that it is a combination of Native American, Anglo-Saxon, and Germanic names given to months that gave birth to the terms commonly used for the full moon today.

This moon is named a "wolf moon," as it is the first full moon of the year. In January, wolves howled in hunger outside Indigenous villages, according to *The Farmer's Almanac*. But in some cultures, this moon was known as Old Moon, Ice Moon, Snow Moon, and the Moon after Yule.

Tonight, too, the fainter stars of the winter constellations and the Milky Way will lighten the night: all those little gems sparkling against the black skin of the sky.

January 23, 2019
Opossum

Yesterday, I attended a workshop in Waterloo called "Care of the Soul." There were three other women in the group and the facilitator. We drew oracle cards from two decks and reflected on them in the sacred circle. We wrote journal entries based on the cards and a philosophy that read: "If you regard blockage as potentially beneficial, you realize that through inconvenience and discomfort growth is promoted." I arrived worried about my mother whose mind seems a little confused lately. I drew the Opossum card from an animal deck of medicine cards. It offered me practical wisdom: "Have a plan. Use common sense. Honour the strategy that works best for you." I reflected on this blurb then found myself writing lists of how to proceed in the future. I studied the imagery on the card: the Opossum, a small rodent-like animal encircled in light, balanced on a branch decorated with a feather, small antlers, a bone and a medicine bag.

A little research when I returned home revealed that the Opossum comes as a spirit guide to offer quick fixes to complicated problems. Moreover, the resourceful Opossum is a trickster. Some of us have heard the old saying "playing Opossum" which refers to a strategy it employs to ward off potential predators. We might assume this creature is "playing dead." But, in fact, the peace-loving animal's nervous system allows it to lapse into a coma-like state when frightened or faced with attackers. It is, therefore, a symbol of master trickery and problem solving.

The Opossum is blind at birth which forces it to develop instincts and senses. It is a guide to honing these skills and to uncovering spiritual truths. It is not surprising, then, that the second card I drew — from the Angelic Messenger Deck — was the Divine Guidance card. I had been feeling abandoned by the spirit world lately and so heaved a sigh of relief that I would be led like a young Opossum through the darkness.

January 25, 2019
Justin 'Beaver'

In August, pop singer Justin Bieber, who has sold an estimated 140 million records, purchased a mansion on over 100 acres of land just off Puslinch Lake, home to much wildlife including beavers. I have friends and family who live in Puslinch, which is a rural area a few minutes from Cambridge where I live. Bieber and his new bride, Hailey Baldwin, will no doubt attract a lot of action on the lake, fans gawking from sea doo jet skis at their 9,000 square foot home which features four bedrooms and six bathrooms. Puslinch has always been a very remote and quiet place, it may become a hub of media attention now.

Perhaps Justin Bieber, who was raised in Stratford Ontario, wishes to return to his Canadian roots. He has been spotted this past summer riding his bicycle around his hometown and enjoying normal activities like getting ice cream. But Bieber, who has been named one of the top ten most powerful celebrities in the world three times by *Forbes* magazine, is not likely to live a simple country life. The Puslinch palace he has purchased for $5 million includes a two-storey wine room, an observatory, a gym and a horseracing track and stables. He might bring a new kind of energy to the Township of Puslinch, whose main sources of production have been agriculture, spring-water bottling and mining. Perhaps the idol will even Twitter about this postage-stamp community to his more than 100 million followers, inciting them to type Puslinch into their GPS devices.

January 28, 2019
Dukkha

The facilitator of the "Care of the Soul" workshop has sent an email and asked the members to reflect on a statement from mystic Ralph Blum: "Through inconvenience and discomfort growth is promoted." In other words, "Challenges provide opportunities that force us to search for a new center of gravity" (Oprah Winfrey).

My challenges have included psychological, spiritual and physical pain, but I have tried over the last few years to remind myself of the Buddha's first teaching: the first Noble Truth. He said, "All I teach is suffering (dukkha) and the end of suffering." Suffering in his view does not necessarily refer to physical pain but rather the mental suffering we experience when we struggle to hold onto pleasure: our lives, our loves, our identities, our possessions...This is dukkha, an experience of basic frustration, discontent, anxiety and despair, due, in part, to believing that eternal happiness can be attained through things that are, in fact, ephemeral and transient.

According to Buddhism, we are trapped in the cycle known as samsara, an endless cycle of birth, death, and rebirth. It is also understood as the world of suffering and dissatisfaction, the opposite of nirvana, which literally means "quenching" or "blowing out." When we extinguish the triple wick of greed, hatred and delusion, we are free from suffering and the cycle of rebirth.

A transformed personality and state of consciousness is characterized by peace, intrinsic joy, compassion, and subtle awareness. These, say the Buddhists, are qualities of an enlightened mind. Saints in many religious traditions developed some, or all, of these qualities, but ordinary people can also release their tight grasp on states of fear, unhappiness and pain.

January 29, 2019
A Salve For Every Sore

In my 20s, I was fortunate enough to study with a number of celebrated Canadian poets: bpNichol, Patrick Lane, Don Coles, Don McKay, Henry Beissel, Miriam Waddington...Many of them were lighthearted in the classroom and supportive of the young, fledgling writers who were struggling to find a poetic voice of their own. When I was 24, I received a full scholarship to the Banff Centre where I spent six indulgent weeks in their Spring Studio, working on my first manuscript and editing it with mentors who polished it to such an extent it was accepted by Cormorant Books and became my first collection: *A Salve For Every Sore*. The program director was the wonderful Jewish writer Adele Wiseman who won the Governor General's Award for her novel *The Sacrifice*, published in 1956. I became friendly with her daughter, Tamara Stone, who is a visual artist. When Adele passed away of cancer a couple of years later, I attended a shiva for her in her little home in the Annex area of Toronto. The mirrors were draped with cloth, as is the Jewish tradition. Tamara sat cross-legged on her mother's bed. A mobile, a kinetic sculpture Tamara had created for her, hung above: weighted objects balanced freely in space. I imagined Adele dying slowly beneath its grace.

February 4, 2019
Year of the Dog

Duchess Kate Middleton's brother, James, recently told the British press that he suffers from depression, an illness he calls a "cancer of the mind." He wrote a personal essay for the *Daily Mail* in which he shares his struggles. He is speaking out about his own experiences, he says, to help reverse the stigma often associated with mental illness. He also wishes to support Heads Together, a mental health initiative spearheaded by The Royal Foundation. His sister Kate and other royals have joined forces to create a campaign to address this stigma. They are changing conversations about mental illness to expel its negative associations. They are also establishing new and innovative programs and services to encourage those struggling with their mental health, including children, to get help. Ironically, James said that he felt completely alone in his feelings and even contemplated suicide. He did not confide in his family because he found it difficult to communicate to those to whom he was closest and loved best. But James also spoke openly about other personal challenges, which include being severely dyslexic as a child and being diagnosed with Attention Deficit Disorder (ADD) last year. Kate's brother, however, does not always regard these as obstacles. He sees the ADD as a gift which accounts for his creativity and originality, as well as his emotional intensity, though he admits he has difficulties with the details of running a business.

James sought treatment a year ago which has been helpful to him. But he also writes in the piece that his five dogs, particularly one called Ella who accompanies him to his sessions, have been key to his recovery. As a result, he and Ella now volunteer with an organization called Pets As Therapy (PAT), and Ella recently became a full-fledged therapy-dog. Research has shown that simply petting a dog can offer a variety of health benefits including decreasing levels of stress hormones, regulating breathing and lowering blood pressure. Petting also releases a hormone associated with bonding and affection in both the person and the dog.

Biography

April Bulmer is an award-winning Canadian writer who has had a dozen books of poetry and prose published. She holds Master's degrees in creative writing, religious studies and theological studies. Some of her books are known for their themes of feminist spirituality. *Year of the Dog: A Poet's Journal* was shortlisted for the International Beverly Prize held by Eyewear Publishing in London, England. *Out of Darkness, Light* (Hidden Brook Press, John B. Lee Signature Series, 2018) and *And With Thy Spirit* (Hidden Brook Press, 2016) were both finalists in the Next Generation Indie Book Awards in the U.S. *The Weight of Wings* (Trout Lily Press, 1997) was shortlisted for the Pat Lowther Memorial Award for the best book of poetry by a Canadian woman. Her work has appeared in such prestigious journals, magazines and newspapers as *The Malahat Review*, *Arc*, *PRISM international*, *Contemporary Verse 2*, *Journal of Feminist Studies in Religion*, *Anglican Theological Review*, *Grand Magazine*, *Toronto Star* and *The Globe and Mail*. Originally from Toronto, where she worked at *Maclean's* magazine and TVOntario, April now lives in Cambridge, Ontario where she won a YWCA Women of Distinction Award in the Arts & Culture category. She is often employed as a poetry judge and is an editor at the online magazine *Devour: Art & Lit* Canada. April writes most days.

More information about April Bulmer can be found at aprilbulmer.wordpress.com.

Other Publications by April Bulmer

Out of Darkness, Light (Hidden Brook Press, John B. Lee Signature Series), 2018

Creeds and Remedies: The Feminine and Religion in Waterloo Region (Serengeti Press), 2017

And With Thy Spirit (Hidden Brook Press), 2016

Women of the Cloth (Black Moss Press), 2013

The Goddess Psalms (Serengeti Press), 2008

Black Blooms (Serengeti Press), 2007

Holy Land (Serengeti Press), 2006

Spring Rain (Serengeti Press), 2004

Oh My Goddess (Serengeti Press), 2004

HIM (Black Moss Press), 1999

The Weight of Wings (Trout Lily Press), 1997

A Salve For Every Sore (Cormorant Books), 1991

www.ingramcontent.com/pod-product-compliance
Lightning Source LLC
Chambersburg PA
CBHW020355170426
43200CB00005B/182